My Goose is Cooked

Hallie's Hands, 1996 ©James Evans 2004

My Goose is Cooked
The Continuation of a West Texas Ranch Woman's Story

Hallie Stillwell

Assembled by Betty Heath

Edited by Kelly S. García

ISBN 0-9707709-2-8
ISBN 978-0-97077-092-9

Center for Big Bend Studies
Occasional Papers No. 9

Robert J. Mallouf, Series Editor
Elaine Robbins, Technical Editor

Cover: Portrait of the Yellow Rose of Texas. Photograph courtesy of the *Ft. Worth Star Telegram* (June 1987).

Chapter-head illustration of the Hallie Stillwell Hall of Fame is by H. T. Miller, Jr., of San Antonio.

In Memory of
Brenda Ann Trudeau

CONTENTS

ACKNOWLEDGMENTS

Betty Heath

I would like to thank the following people for their assistance and encouragement with this book:

First and foremost, thanks to the late Dadie Stillwell Potter. When the Lord created Hallie Stillwell, he did not break the mold. He used it again for Dadie. Thanks also to Dadie's children, Kay Pizzini, Linda Perron, Nannette Patton, and Travis Potter; our cousins Billy and Bill Harrington, friends Roy and Louise Lackey, Steve and Arlene Griffis, Bill Ivey, Richard Bowers, and the late Inda Benson, Hallie's best friend.

Thanks to Kenneth Ragsdale and Russ Gibson for their fond recollections; and to Kathleen Tolbert Ryan and the *Dallas Morning News* for permission to reprint a few of Frank X. Tolbert's columns. Thanks to H. T. Miller Jr. of San Antonio for permission to use the illustration of the museum on the chapter heads. Thanks to Arlene Griffis and Tom Pilkington for their review of the manuscript and comments. I am grateful to Bill Harrington for sharing a number of his mother's photos. Thanks to Gardner Smith for contributions so numerous I couldn't begin to mention them. And thanks to my son Gary and his family, and to friends Jack Heath, Lavinia Lohrmann, and James Stone, for keeping me company on many long trips to the ranch.

PREFACE

When Hallie Crawford Stillwell died on August 18, 1997, she was two months and two days short of her 100th birthday. Hallie had published the first volume of her memoirs in 1991. In that volume she told the story of her life as a pioneer ranch woman and wife in the Big Bend country from the time of her marriage in 1918 to the death of her husband Roy Stillwell in 1948. She titled those memoirs *I'll Gather My Geese* after a saucy reply she made to her father when he told her she was going on a wild goose chase when she signed a contract in 1916 to teach in the border village of Presidio, Texas. At that time Mexican revolutionary Pancho Villa was active along the border. Hallie fulfilled her contract, and the next year she took a teaching job in Marathon, much to the relief of her mother and father. That relief was to be short-lived, for soon the pretty young schoolteacher caught the eye of a handsome widower who was homesteading a spread near the mouth of Maravillas Canyon, some twenty-five miles north of the Mexican border. Stillwell was twice as old as the object of his affections. He raced horses, played poker, and frequently enjoyed a toddy. Hallie's heart fell at his feet. The pair eloped to Alpine and married in the home of her cousin Sadie on July 29, 1918.

"That woman schoolteacher won't last six months down here," Roy's cowhands predicted glumly as they moved their gear to the barn from the luxury of Roy's one-room shack. They were wrong. She lasted seventy-nine years. That's 4,108 weeks, or 28,756 days. And most of those days it didn't rain. Though she lived her last months in a nursing home in Alpine, in her heart, mind, and spirit she was never far from her beloved ranch.

Before Hallie became too infirm to write, she completed ten chapters of the second volume of her memoirs. She herself titled that work *My Goose Is Cooked*.

In 1998 her daughter, Dadie Stillwell Potter, passed the task of completing Hallie's work to me. My grandfather and Hallie were first cousins. Throughout my life we have retained close family ties. My family made spring and autumn visits to the ranch regularly, and Hallie and her family loved to come visit us in Erath County. From my earliest memory, I can recall being put to bed in the next room and listening as the cousins exchanged stories of times past and talked about their current lives and challenges. I certainly never dreamed of how those stories would come to serve me later in life! Hallie was more storyteller than writer, and she did not leave a vast paper trail. Mail to the Big Bend was exceedingly slow in those days, and when Hallie wanted to communicate, she picked up the phone. I have worked with documents from her limited files. And I have worked from my memory, which has gone back far beyond anything I ever expected. After Hallie's ten chapters, this book is a mixture of her writing and mine. I have felt her guiding spirit. I hear her stories told in her voice.

I saw Hallie for the last time in April of 1997. As I walked into her room at the nursing home, she looked up at me and said, "Hello, Treasure. How's Cousin Charlie? Did he come with you?" Treasure was my mother, and she had been dead for eleven years. Cousin Charlie, my grandfather, had been gone fifty-one years. Some say that Hallie lost her mental powers at the end, but it seemed to me that she just rearranged them. The end of the twentieth century was not working well for her, so she retreated into a time when things were more manageable. And that may not be a bad way to go.

Betty Heath
Stephenville, Texas

A Brief Family History

Betty Heath

The Stillwells

John Stillwell, Roy's father, was born near Vicksburg, Mississippi, in 1832, the youngest of three sons. His father died when he was five years old. In those days children were placed in situations where they were taught a trade, a custom called "bounding out." A cousin took John, but the arrangement was not a happy one, so at the age of twelve, he ran away. He wandered the Mississippi bottomland until the captain of a boat going to New Orleans picked him up. John stayed with the captain, who taught him how to manage the boat, until he was twenty-one. After that he worked as overseer for a plantation.

In 1857 John worked on a boat running from the Gulf of Mexico to Victoria, Texas. In 1859 John married Miss Emily Kay of Kempers Bluff, Texas, near Victoria. Two years later, they joined the Box Colony, which had been organized to settle a tract of land granted by the Mexican government near Tampico. The colony was not successful, and eventually disbanded, with the individual families going their separate ways. The Stillwells remained in Mexico for seven years before making their way to Brownsville, where John earned a living transporting freight up and down the Rio Grande. In 1867 the family lived in San Patricio, Texas. They moved to Lagarto, Texas, in Live Oak County, where Robert Roy Stillwell was born on January 11, 1879. From 1880 to 1884 the

Stillwell family, which now consisted of John and Emily and their children, Elizabeth, Lola, John, Alice, Will, Joe, Nellie, Charlie, and Roy, ranched in Bee County near Beeville, Texas.

In 1884 John Stillwell received a land grant from the Mexican government, located twenty-nine miles south of the Rio Grande in Coahuila. Roy was five years old and the move was a complicated one. Roy became too exhausted to complete the trip so he was left with a tribe of Indians who had befriended the family. The Indians were kind and attentive to him. He learned their language and lived on their diet of jerky, mesquite beans, native berries, prickly pear tunas, and pitayas, and in fall and winter they had piñon nuts. Roy was eventually retrieved and moved to Marathon with his mother.

Nellie Stillwell had been sent to Beeville to attend school, but she was not there long when Roy became ill with typhoid fever. Nellie returned home to care for him, and though he was very ill, her faithful care helped him to recover. Sadly, Nellie's resistance had been lowered by the weeks of intensive care she had given to her brother, causing her to fall ill. She died from typhoid fever and was buried at Stillwell Crossing. She was only sixteen years old.

In 1906 Roy Stillwell homesteaded a ranch in Texas about twenty miles from the border where the mouth of Maravillas Canyon meets the Rio Grande. To prove up on his homestead, which he called Dove Mountain, he built two small buildings, two water tanks, and a corral. No fences existed in the area at that time, and the Stillwell cattle grazed the open range. In 1914 Roy added to the Dove Mountain spread by purchasing approximately fifteen sections near Maravillas Creek. He built his headquarters there, and that is where the Stillwell Ranch is still located. During this time Roy maintained a home in Marathon, where his wife and daughter lived. Roy's first wife died in 1916 of appendicitis, and their fifteen-year-old daughter, Ruth, went to live with Roy's sister, Elizabeth, in California. Roy kept the house in Marathon, but continued to live at the ranch.

The Crawfords

The Crawford family came from Scotland before the Revolutionary War. Like the Stillwells, they lived back and forth across borders, these borders being between Scotland and Ireland. They were Scots-Irish, Scottish Protestants who often crossed over into Ireland to avoid supporting the state church of England. Finally three brothers, William, Robert, and Thomson, decided to immigrate to the Americas. Records in the Pulaski County courthouse in Kentucky show the marriage of Robert to Elizabeth Francis on July 24, 1809. On December 31, 1821, a son, James Jefferson, was born to them in the Arkansas Territory. At this time they were living near the mouth of the Big Blue River, which flows into the Red River north of the present city of Paris, Texas.

James Jefferson Crawford married Sarah Francis Gilliam on October 15, 1843. Soon J. J. relocated to Fannin County in the Republic of Texas where he began preparations to move his family. The family moved to Lamar County in 1846. Their ninth and last child, Alvin Guy, was born on December 9, 1865, in Hunt County, Texas.

On January 21, 1892, Guy Crawford married Nancy Evenda Montgomery, who was born October 23, 1872, in Cleburn Parish, Louisiana. Guy and Nancy made their first home in McLennan County, Texas. It was in Waco that their third child, a daughter, was born on October 20, 1897. The proud parents named her Hallie Marie.

Guy and Nancy moved the family to San Angelo in search of a better living and good schools. They tried living in Estancia, in the New Mexico Territory, when other members of the family moved there. But New Mexico didn't suit them, so they moved back to Texas in two wagons. Guy and his son Frank drove the first wagon, followed by daughters Mabel and Hallie at the helm of the second wagon. Mabel and Hallie were then fifteen and twelve years old. The family settled in Alpine and remained residents of the Big Bend area for the rest of their lives.

After teaching in Presidio for a year at the age of eighteen, Hallie Marie Crawford, much to the relief of her family, applied for a teaching position in Marathon and was hired. During her first term of teaching, Hallie met rancher Roy Stillwell. On July 29, 1918, Hallie and Roy eloped to her cousin Sadie's home in Alpine where they were married.

Roy Stillwell died in an accident in 1948 when his truck, loaded with hay, turned over. Hallie, with her sons Roy (Son) and Guy, took over management of the ranch. Guy stayed on the ranch to tend the cattle. Hallie and Son worked many jobs to pull then through drouth and other adversities. As her brothers' health failed, their sister, Dadie Stillwell Potter, bought their interests and ran the ranch with the help of her husband, W. T. Potter, and their children. Son Stillwell died in 1999. Guy, the youngest of the children of Roy and Hallie, lived on the ranch at the site of the old ranch headquarters until he passed away in 2000. Marie Elizabeth "Dadie" Stillwell Potter passed to her heavenly reward during the early morning hours of May 10, 2001. Dadie always said one should get the important things done early before the heat sets in. The Stillwell Ranch goes on, now in the hands of W. T., daughters, Kay Pizzini, Linda Perron, Nannette Patton, and son Travis Potter.

In the final analysis, Roy Stillwell chose well when he picked that unlikely schoolteacher to be his life's companion in that remote and difficult land!

CHRONOLOGY OF HALLIE'S LIFE

Betty Heath

1897   Hallie is born October 20 in Waco, Texas.

1900   Hallie moves to Ozona in Crockett County.

1905   Hallie moves to Tom Green County near San Angelo.

1908   Hallie homesteads with her family in the Estancia Valley of New Mexico.

1910   Hallie shares driving chores with her sister Mabel on move to Alpine.

1916   Graduates Alpine High School; attends Normal School for Teachers and teaches elementary school in Presidio while the Mexican Revolution rages along the border. She carries a *pistola* in her skirts.

1917   Teaches elementary school in Marathon.

1918   Marries Roy Stillwell and moves to the Stillwell Ranch, which is one of the first in the Big Bend to stock registered Herefords.

1919   Roy Walker "Son" Stillwell is born.

1921   Marie Elizabeth "Dadie" Stillwell is born.

1922   Guy Crawford Stillwell is born.

1930   Hallie begins work as correspondent to the *Alpine Avalanche*.

1944   Son is stationed in England; Dadie marries Emeral Martin.

1945   Dadie's daughter Kay is born.

1948   Roy dies in truck accident; Linda is born to Dadie; Hallie and Guy take over ranch. Stillwell cattle are shipped to Colorado; Hallie visits Virginia Madison in New York; Hallie begins work on *How Come It's Called That?*

1949   Nannette is born to Dadie; Guy marries Diane Pierce; Hallie begins forty-year career as lecturer.

1950   Son marries Gwin Kring Roberts; Hallie establishes her wax camp.

1952   Guy Olin "Tige" is born to Guy and Diane.

1953   Marlene is born to Dadie.

1954   Franklin "Frank" Delmar is born to Guy and Diane; Dadie marries W. T. Potter.

1955   Travis Dean Potter is born to Dadie and W. T.

1956   Hallie begins her Ranch News column.

1957   Hallie becomes a stringer for the *Fort Worth Star Telegram* and the *El Paso Times.*

1958   *How Come It's Called That?* co-authored with Virginia Madison is published by the University of New Mexico Press.

1960   Hallie becomes a stringer for the *San Angelo Standard-Times* and the *San Antonio Express.* She becomes a reporter for United Press International and the Associated Press.

1964   Hallie becomes Justice of the Peace for Brewster County.

1967   Hallie judges the first Terlingua Chili Cook-Off.

1968   Hallie is made permanent Queen of the Terlingua Chili Cook-Off.

1978   Hallie retires as Justice of the Peace of Brewster County; she enjoys a vacation in England; returns to the ranch to stay.

1988   Hallie begins to write her memoirs. She completes the years up to 1948 and sends the manuscript to her agent.

1991   Texas A&M University Press publishes *I'll Gather My Geese.* Hallie travels around the state to promote her book. *Texas Monthly* declares her "Grande Dame of Texas" and she is inducted into the National Cowgirl Hall of Fame.

1994   Hallie is inducted into the Texas Woman's Hall of Fame.

1995   Granddaughter Marlene dies on August 12.

1996   Hallie's health fails; she moves to Alpine to be near medical care.

1997   Hallie passes away on August 18. She is buried in Elm Grove Cemetery in Alpine beside her mother and father.

1998   Hallie is inducted into the Texas Heritage Hall of Honor.

Organizations to which Hallie belonged:

- Alpine Pilot Club and Pilot International
- Daughters of the Republic of Texas
- United Daughters of the Confederacy
- American Legion Auxiliary
- Marathon School Board
- Texas Woman's Press
- Big Bend National Park and Development Committee
- West Texas Historical Society
- Brewster County Historical Society

THE LAST TEN CHAPTERS

Hallie passed away before she could complete writing her memoirs. The early years were published in 1991 as I'll Gather My Geese. *This narrative picks up where she left off, in 1948 with the death of her husband Roy.*

Chapter One

A good half-hour before the sun came up over the Stillwell Mountains, my husband Roy was scraping ashes from the stove preparing the morning coffee. I dozed in bed, but I could still hear as he ground the Arbuckle coffee in the grinder that sat on the ranch safe. The smell of the brew was delicious, and I waited for the cup I knew Roy would bring me. I lay in bed with closed eyes so he would have the pleasure of waking me as he always did in the morning.

After his gentle nudge, I took the coffee cup and enjoyed a few minutes before I had to rise. This day would be dusty, hot, and dry as usual. I thought of the troubles ahead and worried about our cattle. I hoped the drouth would soon come to an end.

I listened as Roy puttered in the kitchen and soon smelled the bacon and biscuits. I cuddled my cup in my hands and gave thanks for my life, Roy, our children, and our ranch. Roy did not often treat me to breakfast in bed, so I knew this was going to be one of those special days….

I heard a loud bang in the kitchen and sat straight up in bed. I had no coffee cup in my hand, and Roy was not in the kitchen. There was no one at home but me. I gazed at the sunlight pouring through the windows and knew that reality had taken over. Roy would never be there again, but I savored his memory for a moment, then rose from the bed. One thing I knew was that I had to face life now without the man who was my friend, teacher, and husband. I thought back over his often-repeated advice, "Hallie, you got to be tough if you're gonna make it on this ranch."

I shook out the cobwebs and stretched my arms. I thought to myself, "The rest of 1948 is going to be terrible if things continue this way."

I dressed and headed for the kitchen. I stared at the coffeepot for a long time as thoughts of the past filled my mind. I decided that I didn't want coffee this morning. I wanted my sand dune and my rock. I clomped across the kitchen and out the door. I walked across the desert and perched on my favorite boulder to sort things out. I was a bit dazed. I needed Roy's vision and experience to run our ranch. I could still see Roy mounting Old Red and riding off to tend our cattle. "Our" cattle. It was no longer our cattle, it was "my" cattle. I knew times were going to be tough, but times in the past had been tough. I figured I could do it.

I gazed off at the far blue mountains. Nothing was different, but nothing was the same. I heard something whistling over my head. I looked up and saw a beautiful golden eagle soaring in the clear sky. He banked and flew over my head and shrieked a greeting. I heard a calf cry for its mother. The mother answered. I looked over to the tank and saw our saddle horses going down to drink. They looked so confident and secure. For them, life was simple. A beautiful green collared lizard crossed the sand in search of some shade. It was still early morning but the sun was already fierce. For him life was not so simple. He slithered under a rock just in time to avoid being eaten by a roadrunner. As I watched the desert come to life, I realized that all of us must live one day at a time. All of Roy's plans for the future had come to an end. If there were going to be plans for the future now, they were going to have to be mine. I was not going to give up the ranch.

We had just been favored with a new addition to the Stillwell family. Linda Lou, my daughter Dadie's child, was born just a week after we buried Roy. She deserved the best, as did all my

2

family, and I would see that they all got the most from me. My only thought now, "Today is a new day!"

I rose from my boulder, straightened my shoulders, and marched to the house. I saw my son Guy standing there all discouraged. "Guy!" I called. "We've got work to do, and we're not getting it done moping around here. Saddle up the horses!"

Two weeks had passed since we buried Roy. I knew I could no longer spend all my time mourning for him. Together, our children and I were going to keep the Stillwell Ranch running. Though it would be different now with Roy gone, we would find a way to keep his dream alive. Guy had saddled my horse and was holding my reins for me. I took the reins and mounted, and suddenly I felt Roy's presence. I heard him whisper, "Hallie, life is tough and only the tough survive." I rode off toward the mountains with Guy following close behind. We rode all day, mending our fences, looking for dogies, tending the tanks and windmills, and counting the herd. By sundown we dragged back to the corral. We were exhausted, but Guy, so much like his father, did not complain.

He unsaddled our horses while I fixed some biscuits and beans and peeled an onion. We ate supper in silence and then called it a day. As I crawled in bed I knew I was going to make Roy proud of us. I thought back over the times Roy had been so tough on me, and now I knew that he had been preparing me for this day. I think he must have known that one day I would have to take over his dreams, and he wanted me to know what to do. When he would get disgusted with me, he would say, "When I'm gone you will lose this ranch in six months." I slipped off into sleep knowing Roy was smiling down on us, and I would die before I would give up this ranch. I was not going to lose this ranch in six months. I was never going to lose this ranch!

The next morning I reached for Roy but soon accepted the emptiness of our bed. I got up, dressed, and put the coffee on and started breakfast. Then I woke Guy and told him to get ready for another long day. The smell of bacon frying and coffee brewing brought scenes of happier times to mind, but I pushed them aside. We ate quickly and headed for the barn. The morning was bright, the mountains deep blue, the sky clear, and the desert calm and inviting. I said a silent prayer for rain and mounted my horse. We rode in silence, the heat growing and the dust covering our faces. About noon, I heard some honking above us. There was a flock of geese flying north in their V formation. We watched them until they were completely out of sight in the clear sky. You know when the geese fly north, summer is not long behind.

I longed for clouds. Any kind would do: threatening ones, clouds that pounded with thunder, flashed with lightning, and carried the rain. I had called one truckload of cattle back on the day we shipped most of our herd to Colorado because it rained that day. I had not seen a drop of rain since then. I wondered if I had made a mistake, but I did not share these thoughts with Guy. I wanted him to believe that we could hold the ranch no matter what the circumstance.

April had been a haze of fear, dread, and sorrow. May had slid past with no rain, but Guy and I worked hard every day. June came with no clouds or signs of giving us any moisture. I sent Guy to Colorado to check on the cattle we had shipped out there, so now I rode alone, checking the tanks and watching our cattle get skinnier day by day. July came and still we received no rain, but there was reason to hope. In the Big Bend of Texas most of the rain comes in late summer and early autumn.

One evening early in July I was sitting under our arbor enjoying the shade. I could see heat rising from the shimmering desert. There was no movement anywhere. I hadn't heard from my son Son or daughter Dadie in weeks, but I figured no news was good news. I fanned myself with a greasewood wand and settled into my chair to enjoy the view of the blue mountains. Just then I heard a truck coming down the road. I looked north, and there was a cloud of dust rolling up over Maravillas Creek. I jumped up. From out of the dust cloud came Son's truck pulling a trailer. What was this?

I couldn't believe my eyes. The trailer he was towing was loaded with cattle feed. He pulled past me and headed for the barn. I grabbed the trailer gate and gasped for breath. All Son said was, "Where's Guy? We need to get this feed unloaded."

I yelled out, "Guy! Guy!" He was coming out of the house where he had been resting after a hard day's work. We got that feed unloaded pronto. Our cattle would have a chance.

I looked to the southern mountains across into Mexico and thought how it must have been for Roy's family when they first started ranching this land. Surely they had experienced times

4

worse than these. If they could survive, so could we. At that moment I promised Roy I would hold on to this land!

Chapter Two

The summer of 1948 passed, and we had fed all of Son's feed to our cattle. Life was becoming nightmarish as we watched the parched land grow ever more dry. We were on constant watch for coyotes, eagles, and panthers. If the drouth didn't get our cattle, the predators would.

It had been five months since Roy passed away. Guy had gone out to Colorado to tend the rest of our herd. He wrote that many of our cattle had been lost during the trip. Roy had told me once about how railroad workers handled the stock. He said that crews would often just dump the weakened stock off with the dead.

As I read his letter I knew I had to be smart. I could not let this go unreported. I left the post office in Marathon and headed straight for Alpine to visit my attorney, Frank Ray. I told him my story about the lost cattle.

Ray asked, "How did you ship them?" I told him that we had used Santa Fe Railway, and they had assured me of good passage. Ray looked at me and said, "I can't represent you because I have been Santa Fe's attorney for years."

He also told me that if I filed against the Santa Fe, he would be representing them and fighting me. This really put a damper on my mood.

I knew no other attorney and had no other person to turn to. Roy had always been stern about not showing much emotion. Just as I reached my car, I bumped into an old friend from Marathon, Dick Arnold.

I just started pouring out my story right there on the sidewalk. I told him everything from Roy's death to the present. He listened as I babbled. He told me there was always more than one way to skin a cat. He said, "Go over to the Santa Fe office and talk to the agent, Dennis Brown. He will give you a form to fill out." I nodded. "Now, Hallie, you need to fill out this claim as though you lost twice as many cattle as you really did—this is just customary. The railroad will cover only one-half of the cost of losses, and you'll be lucky to get that!"

I thanked him for his advice. I wiped my face, straightened my shoulders, and marched over to the Santa Fe office. Before I was a quarter of the way through my argument, Dennis handed me a form and asked me to fill it out. When I got to the number of cattle lost, I thought about what Dick Arnold had said. Then I heard Roy's voice, "Tell the truth, pay your debts, and keep your credit good!" I filled in the forms with exactly the number of cattle I had lost. I turned in the form and walked out with my head held high. I had been honest just as Roy would have been. I also knew I would probably get very little in compensation because of it.

I did not expect a response from the railroad. I went back to work. About a week after meeting with Frank Ray, our mail carrier gave me a note from him, which summoned me to his office. We did not get mail at the ranch but once a week, so I immediately drove to Alpine, over a hundred miles away. When I got to his office, he introduced me to two lawyers from Amarillo. Bill Tilton was also there to act as advisor for the Santa Fe Railway. Suddenly I was facing four stern men gathered behind a massive desk. They nodded for me to sit on the opposite side. With a certain amount of trepidation, I watched one of the lawyers thumb through the papers. He began to question me. This went on for nearly three hours. They repeated questions frequently and reminded me of the railroad policy of one-half recovery of losses. Well, I certainly knew that half recovery would not be enough.

Eventually one lawyer asked, "What kind of proof do you have of your losses?" Well, I had no proof. I just knew what my cattle were worth and how many I had lost. I could only tell the truth. I gave them the exact number I had lost.

They looked at each other, shook their heads, and one of them said, "Okay, you win! Let's go to lunch!" I wasn't sure what I had won, but I went to lunch with them.

Afterward I drove back to the ranch, wondering when I would receive the check for damages, but I was determined not to worry about it. I carried out the ranch chores for the rest of the week, and on Saturday I went up to Marathon. I got my mail, expecting a letter from Guy, when I spotted a letter with the Santa Fe Railway logo. My hands were trembling as I opened it. I could hardly believe my eyes! Mr. Ray had advised the company that had the matter gone to trial, any jury in Brewster County would have awarded me the full amount! I knew Roy would have been proud of me. That certainly was a lot of money in those days.

Now that I had the check for damages and knew that the rest of the cattle were safe and well fed in Colorado, I began to enjoy the ranching business again. Guy came home at the end of July, and I had hired a Mexican man to help on the ranch. Things were beginning to fall into place. We had plenty of everything but rain.

While I was enjoying this time at the ranch, I received a letter from my friend Virginia Madison. We first met in 1947, the year before Roy died. She had come to the ranch to interview him about some place names in the Big Bend. Roy was fond of her and observed that she was "as pretty as a speckled pup." Not many people could fit in with Roy, but Virginia got along well with him, and he gave her all kinds of historical information. She was delighted. In no time at all we were firm friends.

Later Virginia told me that she had been warned about Roy's taciturn nature. Some said that he would not give her the time of day, but Roy enjoyed talking with her, and he told her a lot about things in the Big Bend that even I had never known. Roy basked in our attention. I gained a lot of new knowledge, and Virginia left with more information than she had expected. Virginia and I continued our friendship for many years through correspondence.

This new letter was rather shocking. She asked me to help her write a book on the place names of the Big Bend and invited me to visit her in New York. Since her husband Dick Madison had to go to California on a business trip, we would be able to spend the time he was away organizing the book.

I didn't need to think too long about it! Things were running smoothly at the ranch, and we had begun to have some evening showers. Rain usually comes in July, and this year August was forming up to expectations.

I went up to Marathon to make train reservations. The ticket agent told me that it was not an easy trip from Marathon to New York, so I decided I would go over to Alpine to see my friend Louie Starns, who was the Southern Pacific ticket agent there. He told me that the trains were fully booked for some time to come, but that he would do what he could, and told me to go back home.

He would call me on the phone as soon as he could arrange something.

The next day I was hanging laundry on the line when the telephone rang. Virginia Madison was calling. She was beside herself with excitement. She told me that she had been invited to an important party and that she wanted me to go with her. She said that we would meet several people who could help us with the publication of our book. She pleaded with me to make reservations right away. I hung up the phone and jumped in the car and drove as fast as the law allowed back over to Alpine to see Louie. I told him I was willing to ride in a boxcar if necessary, but that he had to get me on an eastbound train somehow.

Louie took one look at me and knew there would be no stopping me. He sighed and said, "Okay, go get your luggage and be back as soon as possible. I'll find a way." It didn't take long for me to get to Marathon, pack my things, and return. Before I left I scribbled a note to Guy. I knew he would fuss about the trip. None of my children wanted me to travel alone, especially on such a long trip. But I was going to New York no matter what. My head was spinning. This poor country girl was going to get on the next train to New York City!

As I sat on one of those hard benches at the station, I wondered what Roy would think about my leaving the ranch this way. Somehow I knew he would approve. The ranch was doing as well as could be expected considering the drouth. I could not make the sky produce rain, so my trip to New York was something I was going to do for myself. It had been a long time since I had done anything for me. The ranch had consumed my entire body, mind, and soul since Roy died.

Louie called out my name. He told me that a Southern Pacific passenger train had just passed through Marfa and was heading up Paisano Pass. From there it was downhill to Alpine. It would arrive shortly. And I had a ticket to ride.

Soon we heard a not-so-distant whistle and Louie stepped from behind the ticket counter to help me with my luggage. The train pulled into the station blowing smoke and steam. He ushered me to the train and introduced me to the conductor who was an old friend of his. Louie told him, "Now that change in New Orleans is a little difficult. Please help Mrs. Stillwell out if you can." I felt decidedly queasy. I had never been anywhere other than the prairies of New Mexico and Texas. All of a sudden I wasn't feeling so brassy anymore. Nevertheless, I settled in my seat. The train whistled and lurched forward. For better or worse I was off on my great adventure. I watched Alpine fall behind, and the great Big Bend landscape, so familiar to me since I was a young girl, pass before my eyes. "New York City," I said out loud, "here comes Hallie Stillwell, ranch woman."

Chapter Three

So much had happened since Roy's death. I had been too busy and too worried about the future to think much about it, but now as I sat on the train and watched the countryside roll by, I had the leisure to think back about it all. The train was crowded and people were moving about as though it was a busy city street. People nodded politely and smiled as they passed me. Many of them were generous and helpful to me. Soon I discovered I was being treated like a queen. Stories I had heard from friends about train travel were nothing like this! At first I just thought folks were taking pity on a rube, but it did not take long to discount this theory.

Two women from Mission, Texas, noticed all the attention I was getting and came up to talk. They said I must be someone important due to all the service I was getting. I told them I was Hallie Stillwell. Immediately they nodded in recognition and gasped, "Oh, so you are the Widow Stillwell." Well, yes, I nodded, and they returned to their seats, whispering all the way. I wondered how they knew Roy had passed away, but I gave it little more thought. I just enjoyed all the nice people who were stopping by to chat with me. Everyone was so friendly, and I spent much of my trip talking with people from all parts of the country.

The train pulled out at four in the afternoon and we traveled all through the night. Surprisingly I had no difficulty sleeping, and I actually enjoyed the sounds of the rail wheels on the tracks and the sound of the steam whistle blowing at the many road crossings. I had often watched the trains passing through Alpine and Marathon, and now I was riding one. Moreover I was actually sleeping on one!

I awoke refreshed to the sunrise pouring through the windows, and dressed in far more leisurely fashion than I ever did on the ranch. I made my way forward to the dining car. There I was promptly attended, and I enjoyed a luxurious breakfast. Coffee tastes so much better when you don't have to make it yourself! Once again people whispered around me and no one failed to wish me a good morning. Well, I supposed the world outside West Texas must be a friendlier place than I thought.

We arrived in New Orleans around mid-morning. The train station was more crowded than I thought possible. This was unbelievable. I had always heard about New Orleans, but I never dreamed I'd see it. I gathered the luggage and stepped off the train, momentarily confused.

A man came up and asked if I was Mrs. Stillwell. Sure enough, I said, and he asked me to come with him. This was a little forward, I thought, but I went with him, and we boarded a bus. He explained that he was a railroad agent, and that I had a little time before my next train departed, so he thought I might like to see the town. Well twist my arm, son! I felt as if I was getting the grand tour. This was so much better than sitting around that old train station for hours, and he was such a gentleman. I have always felt that Texans are the friendliest people in the world, but these New Orleans folks were matching us and then some. After an hour of touring, we arrived at the Roosevelt Hotel in downtown New Orleans.

He thought I would enjoy waiting in the lobby of this grand hotel. I would not need to get a room because I had only a few hours before my next train. When the hotel manager learned that I was the Widow Stillwell, he gave me a fine free dinner at the restaurant. What Southern hospitality!

While I was dining, a Southern Pacific Railway man approached me. He asked, "Is there anything you would like to do while you are in New Orleans?" I said that I would love to see whatever I could in the time I had before I had to catch my train. But I did not want to miss that train! He said that when I finished my meal he would call a cab. He gave directions to the driver and off we went.

I saw the cemetery where Huey P. Long was buried and the gorgeous cathedral in the center of town. I soaked up every picture in my mind, as I knew this would be the one and only time I would get to see such splendor. The tour lasted two hours, and then the driver returned me to the depot just in time. My train was pulling into the station. He grabbed my luggage and escorted me to the train, where there were a great many people waiting in line. He guided me to the head of the line and right onto the train. I wondered why I was being allowed to board before the others, but I really didn't have time to ask. He helped me up the steps, tipped his hat, wished me a safe journey and then departed. I waved good-bye to him and marveled at the attention I was getting. I couldn't believe how nice all these people were.

The trip north from New Orleans was pleasant. There was beautiful green country, rolling hills, magnificent stallions romping in lush meadows. I caught myself wishing some of the green could be transplanted to Texas. At home I woke every morning to sage, cactus, and desert. Suddenly I was homesick. As beautiful as this land was, I wouldn't trade my home for any of it.

The train ride was comfortable. I spent another night in peaceful sleep. If anything, the attention I was getting was more profound. I couldn't have asked for anything more. I savored every minute I spent on that train. I found myself wishing the trip to New York would never end. Nevertheless we arrived at Pennsylvania Station in New York around noon the following day. I looked at all the people standing around and searched for a familiar face in the crowd. I was a little anxious. There were more people at the train station than in all of Brewster County! I gathered my things up and reluctantly left behind all of the comforts of the train I had enjoyed for three days. The conductor helped me down and wished me well. He asked me if I had friends coming to meet me, and I assured him that I did. But I looked everywhere and did not see them. After a few moments of panic, I spotted Virginia and Dick Madison waving at me. Well, I was mighty glad to see them. They made their way toward me through the crowd. We hugged each other furiously. I turned to thank the conductor who was still hovering close by. He wanted to be sure I was taken care of because he knew I didn't have any idea of what to do or where to go.

Virginia and Dick were full of questions about my trip. They wanted to know everything. I told them of the wonderful people on the train and my adventures in New Orleans. I said I was treated like a queen, but I felt it was because I was such a poor-looking country girl. They laughed and Virginia said, "Oh, no! It was your distinguished appearance and your West Texas smile that got them."

Knowing I was probably a great deal more right than she was, I thanked her anyway. Dick drove through the busy streets as though there was no one else on the road. I felt like I was on a racetrack with way too many cars in the race. I didn't even have time to goggle at the tall buildings or take in the famous places we were passing. As we drove, Virginia talked enthusiastically about our Texas place-name book and the things we had to do in the days ahead. All of it made my head spin!

It took about an hour for us to get from Penn Station to the Madison's apartment in Peter Cooper Village in downtown Manhattan. Their apartment was beautiful. They had furnished it with lovely antiques from all over the country. Virginia was an elegant person, and the apartment's decor reflected her style. I could not imagine such furnishings in West Texas, and least of all, Roy or a cowhand being comfortable in it.

After getting settled in and rested, Virginia outlined the plans for my visit. She wasn't going to allow me to miss a single sight. The first thing on the agenda was a trip to Lyon's Falls in upper New York. We boarded another train, and this one certainly did not have such attentive employees as the Southern Pacific, but we got there comfortably and safely.

Our hostess lived in an old castle in Lyon's Falls. Once settled, we roamed around like children in a fairy tale. The owner was eccentric and well educated. She had attended conservatories in France and England, and she frequently entertained guests with her piano playing and singing. After her entertainment, we had an elegant dinner and then retired to our rooms. I marveled at the size of my room and its opulent furnishings. I doubted any princess had enjoyed better. I undressed, put on my nightclothes, and settled into a feather bed, the luxury of which exceeded anything I had ever dreamed about. Just about the time I started to drift off to sleep, the wind whistled, the walls whispered, and the floors began to creak. I sat straight up in bed, lit the candle, and examined the room. There was nothing unusual, but I couldn't get into a comfortable night's sleep. My night was filled with strange dreams of dragons and knights. I certainly was glad to see the sunrise come. I did not envy our hostess her palatial dwelling or her beautiful furnishings.

While we were there, we ate at several restaurants and even attended a Lion's Club meeting. The countryside was so beautiful and filled with grand mansions. I felt as though I was in a well-tended garden that flowed in rolling hills for miles. I had no idea that a place such as this existed except in the works of fiction. It was a dreamland of mystery to someone who came from a land with miles and miles of desert!

I asked Virginia about the woman who owned the castle. She told me that the woman was at one time very wealthy due to an inheritance, but over the years she spent most of the money. She refused to sell the castle and worked to keep it presentable, but now she lived in the servant's quarters because she could not afford the luxury of operating it at full capacity. Yet, she always allowed her guests the pleasure of staying in its opulent rooms. No one understood her, but they all enjoyed her parties.

I can truthfully say the trip was wonderful, but still it was bewildering. It was hard for me to believe that one woman lived alone in such a grand place. I was glad when we took our leave. The lights of New York City were welcome, and Virginia's apartment with its noisy street sounds and flashing neon lights were a relief from that strange weekend.

We began a new round of activities. Back in Marathon and Alpine, you just didn't fail to speak to folks as you passed them on the street. I fairly wore myself out the first few days trying to greet everyone I passed. Finally I had to give it up in the interest of getting to our destination. I just hoped those city folks would not find my manners lacking! We attended the theater, went shopping, toured the museums, and even attended a Chinese wedding. A young couple from prominent families was getting married. It was the event of the year. Even the mayor of New York attended. Dick, Virginia, and I were treated as honored guests and were seated next to the bride's family. The finery was magnificent and the traditions delightful to watch. At the reception, we placed ourselves in the foyer to cool off. People lined up to shake our hands and congratulate us. It took awhile before we realized we were at the end of the receiving line and being considered family. We loved it!

Dick Madison was an economist for the Texas Oil Company, located in the Chrysler Building in New York. There was not much he couldn't get accomplished, so I was treated to royal tours of the city and state. I had a wonderful time while I was there thanks to the friendship Roy had established with Virginia. It always seemed that Roy would be a part of me no matter where I went or what I did.

Dick could get tickets to all the shows, off and on Broadway. We saw *South Pacific, Mr. Roberts,* and *Hello, Dolly.* I was entertained every single night I was in New York. I walked in the rain, ran through the department stores, shopped until I dropped, and then got up and shopped again. If ever there was a country girl gone to town, I was she.

I began to wonder how Virginia got interested in the Big Bend of Texas. She told me that she had attended Sul Ross College in Alpine, where she had earned her Bachelor and Master's degrees. During those years she explored much of the Big Bend country. She fell in love with the landscape, the wide variety of desert plants and animals, and she came to wonder how all of the landmarks had been named. There were the Chisos Mountains, Presidio, Stillwell Crossing, Dove Mountain, Black Gap, Dead Horse Mountains, Maravillas Canyon and Creek, Boquillas, Pack Saddle Mountain, Dog Canyon, Dagger Flat, Rosillos Mountains, Study Butte, Terlingua, and many others.

Virginia diligently wrote everything down as I explained about all the names of the places. We worked well together because we loved the same things. The more we talked, the more we learned. The more we learned, the more excited we became. It soon became apparent that we had the makings of a book after all. Not only was Virginia becoming a dear friend, she now was going to be my co-author. For days on end we worked on the book. It seemed to me that writing a book was a lot like running a ranch. No detail was too small to take notice of.

Well, all things come to an end, and so did my visit to New York. I had to head back to Texas, the ranch, and my family. I had been in New York for a month, but it seemed like a day. I dragged through the preparations for the trip. Virginia was blue, too. We sulked around the whole last day, putting off the good-byes until the last minute at the train.

Virginia and Dick waved as my train pulled away from Pennsylvania Station. Something told me this was an experience that would never come again.

My treatment was just as considerate as it had been on the trip east, and I was still puzzled over the special attention. I was escorted onto the train and doted over the entire trip. Though I did not understand it, I decided to relax and enjoy it. In three days I would be back to the toils and troubles of running a West Texas ranch in time of drouth.

The trip home was most pleasurable and uneventful. We transferred in New Orleans with just a short layover. As I waited for the train, I could hardly believe I had done so much in such a short time.

As the train rolled into view of the West Texas mountains, I wondered if there were blue mountains anywhere else in the world. These mountains are not just blue — they are magnificently azure. As the blue peaks came into sight, I knew I was close to home. When I got to Alpine, I went directly to Louie Starn's office and thanked him for the wonderful experience. I told him I was treated like royalty the entire trip. I wanted him to know how much I appreciated his asking others to help me.

Louie began to laugh. I looked at him uneasily, and he told me his story. He said that a few days ago he visited a friend who is a conductor. He asked him if he had taken good care of Hallie Stillwell. He said that they showed you a fine time in New Orleans, how they didn't charge you for any extras, and how they assisted you on the trip to New York. I thanked him and said you would be grateful for their help. With a big grin, Louie continued, "Hallie, the conductor then said, 'We were more than happy to escort and assist the widow of General Joseph P. Stilwell'."

I was astounded. I looked at Louie for a moment and broke out laughing. I had been an impostor for a month and didn't even know it.

Louie said, "No one will hear it from me." I'll bet Roy was laughing with us from across the great divide.

Chapter Four

After my return from New York, I could see further ahead before we rang in 1949. Things weren't getting any easier, I tell you what. The comforting feeling I had upon my return to West Texas was fading fast.

While I was away Guy had returned to Colorado and left our Mexican *segundo* in charge. Also, Son had moved to Oregon to look for work because he could not find enough work in Tornillo.

In Oregon he was working as a logger. That was a dangerous occupation, and Son was just a country boy. So that nagged at me.

Fortunately our *segundo* had taken good care of the place with everyone gone. For several days I rode out with him every morning. We checked cattle, water, and grass. Things were improving, and I was much happier after my trip to New York. I had hope that things would be normal again. Maybe someday we could bring our cattle home from Colorado.

A week at the ranch put things in good shape. We had some rain showers, but not nearly enough to restore the grass our cattle needed. I had been back at the ranch for a week or so when I drove up to Marathon to get the mail. I had planned to return quickly, but I had a letter from Dad and Mother Benson, who had set up the pasturage for our herd in Colorado. They wanted me to come visit. I wanted to go, but I had just been away from the ranch for a month in New York and wondered if the ranch could afford to have me gone for yet another month. Still, I missed Guy, and I felt I needed to see how those cattle were fattening up. I seldom ponder any length of time over decisions. I decided to go.

I telephoned Mother Benson right off and told her I was coming. She said, "Get hold of Gene and Sis (her son and daughter-in-law in Alpine) and come with them. They should be leaving within the next four days." That was welcome news, for I would not have to travel alone. I called them up, and they were happy that I would be joining them on the trip. In just two days I was on the road again.

We traveled through some dry flat country from Alpine to Amarillo, where we stopped for the night. The next morning we started early and soon found ourselves in much prettier country as we crossed into New Mexico.

I marveled at the grassy pastures and the majestic Sangre de Cristo Mountains on the horizon. Cattle along the way looked fat and healthy. I hoped that I would find our cattle faring as well. I wondered how the areas could be so different and yet so much alike. All around me were mountains that reminded me of home. There was much more grass, and as we climbed into Raton Pass there were many more trees. I began to understand what Guy was writing in his letters. Reading between the lines, I could tell he was homesick, yet he wrote of how much the country was like the Big Bend. He knew our cattle were much better off in Colorado, but he preferred to be at home. I was experiencing much of the same feeling as we arrived in Colorado Springs, where Dad and Mother Benson lived.

The Bensons quickly settled me in and made me comfortable. They fed me and let me turn in early after the long trip. They were wonderful hosts, and I will always be grateful for their generosity and hospitality.

While I was in Colorado Springs, Guy came in from Simla where the cattle were pastured, and we all had great fun. The Bensons took us to the various historical places in the area. We spent an enjoyable two weeks, but then it came time to get down to business.

The Bensons had told us about the rough, cold Colorado winters and explained that our cattle would be in danger if we left them in Simla with no one to feed and take care of them. I told Guy that we could not take the herd home yet, for the rains had not produced enough grass to feed all of them. We decided to sell some of them. The Bensons said they would help us. Working cattle in Colorado was difficult even when the weather was good, but working in freezing weather would be even more difficult. Within two days we were ready to move our cattle to market.

First we gathered the cattle. That took about three days. From Simla, we had to drive the herd to the auction blocks in Colorado Springs, no easy task. We all rode horseback and suffered the consequences with soreness. The cattle probably fared better than we did. We lost no cattle, but I lost some inches off my behind. But that loss I could afford.

Once we were at the auction blocks, Dad Benson and I worked the scales while the rest of the men tended the cattle in the pens. Gene was constantly reminding us to watch the scales, as there were often crooked buyers who would jimmy the scales, distract you while weights were gauged, or lie about the poundage. I was determined to get full price for my cattle and not let anyone skim off my profit.

As the cattle came through the chutes, I realized that many had not weathered as well as others while in Colorado. We decided to sell only the fattest and strongest cattle. I had at least a hundred head that had not fattened up at all. They needed more time, and I did not want to sell them at a loss. So we kept them, but I didn't quite know how we were going to go about doing it. I had the auction pens hold my cattle until we decided what to do. They were just pitiful—candidates for the glue factory. I had received a letter from Son who was in Baker, Oregon. He wrote that he had found a ranch up there that would be perfect for raising cattle. It was covered in tall grass and had plenty of water. Moreover, the price was reasonable. He wanted us to buy the ranch and ship the cattle to him. Suddenly I knew we had the answer to our problem, but I would have to go to Oregon. I was one travelin' gal these days.

I asked Gene to go up there with me, and he gladly agreed. We made the trip in two days. Son's ranch was a beautiful place and certainly made for livestock grazing. Gene agreed that the price was right and that we should take advantage of the deal. Son took us to meet Sam Coon, the owner. He agreed to accept $10,000 down and carry the rest of the note. The ranch consisted of two sections (1,280 acres) of mountain pasture and two sections of meadowland bordering the river. I knew I couldn't go wrong if I purchased this land.

I called George Baines in Alpine, who was then president of the First National Bank. You know telephones back then were not what they are now. One often got a poor connection. I could barely hear George's voice. It was as if I was hooked up to a tin can with a cord. I began shouting for fear he couldn't hear me all the way from Oregon.

It turned out that he could hear me just fine, but still I shouted. "I want to buy a ranch!"

"Hallie," he said, "stop shouting, and where are you anyway?"

I told him I was in Oregon and that I had found a way to save our cattle. He was skeptical and asked a lot of questions.

"George, I know what I'm doing. Do I get the money or what?"

He hemmed and hawed for a while, the way all bankers do, but finally he told me to go ahead and write the check.

Well lady, it's too late now, I thought. I hoped Roy was grinning in heaven.

We closed the deal on the ranch, and soon I relaxed. I knew we had a place for our cattle. I thought about those cattle and where they had been—from Dove Mountain to Black Gap, from Black Gap to Marathon, from Marathon to Colorado, and now from Colorado to Oregon. They were almost as well traveled as I was. And we had something else in common. We all had the Stillwell brand!

Chapter Five

Time had passed so quickly, and so much had happened that I had little time to worry. Most of what we had done was spontaneous and for survival. Now we would be expanding our business across the United States, but we were still "in the ring."

While we were in Oregon our cattle in Colorado had improved somewhat. We made plans to move them to Oregon on the railroad. Because we had to drive the herd from one part of Colorado Springs to the railway outside town, we needed some help. Dad and Mother Benson soon found plenty of volunteers who came to our rescue. Some of us formed a wing with our cars near the loading pens to direct the herd into the loading chutes. In no time the cattle were loaded in the cars and on their way. Son was to live in Oregon and raise the cattle. Guy and I wished him well and returned to the ranch in Texas.

As we drove from Marathon to the ranch on that late August day, I realized that we had made the right decision. Our land was empty, desolate and barren. The drouth had continued without cease. Wolves and mountain lions preyed upon the few cattle we had kept on the ranch. During this time, many ranchers who were forced out of running cattle turned to government trapping as a means of survival. Each trapper was paid for the tails and paws of animals caught and killed on ranches that were plagued with an increasing number of predators. Ranchers were begging for trappers, and often there were more offers than there were trappers. We were helpless to the predators' nightly raids, and almost daily we found the corpse of one of our herd. We didn't have the luxury of having one of the trappers, so we had to take care of our own. We instructed our foreman to set traps, and we shot at coyotes, foxes, and wolves, but we scarcely made a dent in the predator population.

Among these predators was the golden eagle. He, too, attacked our small or newborn calves, dealing instant death to his defenseless prey. Losing the baby calves was the hardest thing for me to accept because I knew they were the future of our ranch. We tried hard to keep them alive, and many times we brought the newborns to the house trap for protection.

As August passed and still no rains came, the dryness cracked my face and even my heart. When I rode horseback, I covered myself in hat, gloves, and a long-sleeved shirt. My eyes burned, my ears filled with sand pellets, and my mouth was always dry. Slowly I watched the Big Bend turn into a hell on this earth. Our cattle were starving and their rib bones creaked as they searched for grass. Even the greasewood drooped and dropped leaves from its branches. The sun, the hot blistering sun, was relentless in its fury.

This went on through September and October. Son was having problems in Oregon, too. As we suffered through the drouth, he was seeing the beginning of a severe winter. By October snow covered the entire Oregon ranch. By November we were hearing about the worst winter in years throughout the western United States. At night I sat by the radio and listened for some good news about the weather in Oregon. But the news was always about the blizzards. Many people were freezing. Where our ranch was located, some could not be reached or rescued in days of thirty and forty degrees below zero. I even heard a report about a man who walked out into the snow and was never seen again. As for us in the Big Bend, pressure was mounting. Our feed was running low, money was running out, and the predators were winning the range war. Nevertheless I stuck to my guns and looked for the light at the end of the tunnel.

By December the government was helping the ranchers of the Northwest. Operation Haylift was created. Planes flew over areas where snow made travel by roads impassable. They dropped thousands of bales of hay to starving cattle. I could only hope that our cattle were receiving some of that feed. In mid-December I had a letter from Son. My hands shook as I opened it. I was relieved to see his handwriting, but I feared the news about the cattle would be bad. I was relieved to learn that he had stockpiled plenty of hay for even a severe winter. Still, he wrote that the winter had been so cold that he could accomplish little beyond keeping the cattle fed. Ice and snow covered the land, and the lakes and streams were frozen solid. He stayed indoors most of the time and read by the fireplace.

Two weeks later I got another letter from Son telling me that some of our cattle had died. One day they were fine and the next day they were dead. He checked them over carefully. They were fat and had good coats. He was at a loss to tell what was happening. He asked a neighbor for help. After inspection of the cattle, this neighbor told Son that his cattle were dying from thirst. They could not get to water because of the thick ice. There was plenty of snow, he explained, but it was so cold it burned their tongues. Well, this certainly was a revelation to a boy who grew up in the Chihuahuan Desert! Son had just assumed that as long as there was snow there would be water. He learned quickly what to do and rescued the remaining cattle. He would go out every day and cut a large hole in the ice near the banks of the stream. Soon the cattle figured out that they could drink from this hole. Of course the holes froze over every night, so Son had to do this task daily.

Son learned that on really cold days—temperatures below zero—he would have to dig out the holes and carry water to troughs for the herd. There he would have to keep stirring the water with a pole so it would not freeze. He also knew that he couldn't force the stock to drink, so there were times when this didn't work. He found a spring-fed waterhole where the natural water was warm and remained unfrozen. He drove the cattle there several times to get water when all other methods failed. No more Stillwell cattle were lost for lack of water. No matter where you live, I say, it pays to have good neighbors.

I did not hear from Son again until the middle of February when he wrote that he had survived several ice storms where the ice had pelted him down to the ground and winds had blown him over. This had to be a strong wind because Son stood six-feet, seven-inches tall and weighed 260 pounds back in those days. Despite all obstacles, the cattle were okay, he reported. This was the best news I had all winter. Still I realized that all of us were walking on thin ice, so to speak.

In March, Son wrote that everything was pointing to a good spring. He said the earth was warm again and grass was sprouting everywhere. The snow was melting and the rivers were rising. I rejoiced. Considering what might have happened we had suffered little loss in Oregon and little loss in Texas. I thanked God for that.

On the home ranch Guy was hauling water every day for our cattle. We burned prickly pear so the herd could eat without getting stickers in their mouths. We had feed when we could afford it through the dry winter. By March our herd was thin and bony, but it was alive.

My two sons had proved to be vital to keeping our ranching business alive. From the southwestern border of the Rio Grande to the northwestern border of the United States, we had kept Roy's dream alive!

Chapter Six

By the time 1949 had begun, our lives had really changed. Dadie was living on the Martin Ranch with Emeral, her husband, and baby daughters Emily Kay and Linda. Dadie's third daughter, Nannette, was born in July. Nannette was afflicted with cerebral palsy due to complications from a premature birth. Dadie and Nannette moved into Alpine to be close to her doctor. This separation put stress on her marriage. She slept little at night, worried about Emeral during the day, and tried to keep some sort of family life going, but it was not easy.

The situation on the ranch was not easy either. Finances became more and more strained. Once again, the bank would help feed the cattle but not the people. If we were going to enjoy another day of beans and bacon, something would have to happen pronto. I have observed many times in my long life that help often comes at the last possible moment.

Glen Wilson was a classmate of mine living in San Antonio. At that time Mr. and Mrs. Frank Akerman were visiting him. The Akermans lectured and traveled throughout the United States. They presented travelogues and often spoke about business ventures. Glen told me about them and encouraged them to come to the Big Bend to visit me on the ranch. Glen told them I had plenty of good stories to tell.

The Akermans arrived on a hot and dusty day. I watched their rooster-tail of dust for miles. It was easy to tell when visitors were coming in those days. Today, of course, our roads are paved, and our visitors often fly in and land on the highway.

When the Akermans got out of their car, I asked them to join me under the arbor. I had made a big pitcher of lemonade. We sat for hours talking about many subjects. They were delightful people. I asked them to stay overnight, and their visit turned into a two-week stint of great talks and fine adventures. We walked through the Maravillas Canyon to explore the Indian pictographs and cave dwellings. We visited Big Bend National Park. The park was still pretty new in those days, and it was located to the west just across the Dead Horse Mountains. We even climbed Stillwell Mountain. Mr. Akerman listened to all the stories I had to tell about Roy and me and our life together. He loved hearing me tell about how I bungled and messed up, and how Roy always managed to turn those events into a lesson for me about coping with ranch life.

Frank had become a great appreciator of my lemonade, and one evening while we were enjoying a glass under the arbor after a tiring day, he told me that I should become a public speaker, and as a matter of fact, he would line up a number of engagements for me. He said I could make good money from this work. I was no stranger to work, but I wasn't making any money at it. So I agreed to try this. I had never talked before any group of people. We tossed the idea around every evening over lemonade. Finally we made some definite plans.

When I discussed the deal with my children, they thought I was crazy. They didn't want me driving around the country alone and on my own. But not one of them was willing to go with me. Well, I understood. We were all totally occupied with just trying to stay afloat. I smiled, listened attentively to them, and made my plans. I think they knew in their hearts that the argument was over. But they yammered on that I would be stranded on the road in the night somewhere and be murdered or worse.

In September I loaded up the car and set out for Kentucky. Guy and Dadie just stood and watched. They were speechless. I watched them in the rear view mirror until I couldn't see them any longer. I'm sure they were in shock. Mama was footloose again!

I drove that old car alone all the way to Williamsburg, Kentucky, in two days, stopping only to eat and gas up. I had little money, so I slept in the car. I did stop at a truck stop once to take a shower. Though it was rather tiring, and not at all like my train trips, I did enjoy seeing a different country.

When I got to Williamsburg, I found that Mr. Akerman had booked me at several places across Kentucky. I hardly had gotten my car unloaded when he started talking about my programs. He trained me for several days in public speaking. He suggested things people would be interested in hearing and told me how I could appeal to audiences. I practiced speaking before him and Mrs. Akerman several times. But I feared that practicing before them was not as preparatory as he thought it would be. I wished I could have more training before jumping out on my own.

We began to assemble my props. I had brought with me some things that were common to West Texas ranching. I had branding irons, western wear, spurs, rope, arrowheads, and even my gun. Mr. Akerman gave me the schedule. Within a week I was off again and on my own.

Before I left, Mr. Akerman told me that if I could please the president of the college where I was to speak first, I would have it made. As I drove along these unfamiliar roads, I rode a roller coaster of confidence and insecurity. After a seven-hour drive, I pulled into the college. I found the administration building, but I drove around for ten minutes trying to find a parking place. Eventually I was ushered into a beautiful office where I met the president of the college. He escorted me to a large auditorium and showed me the stage where I would speak. We talked about where I would stand, and he told me where the speakers were and explained about the acoustics. He asked me about how long I was going to talk. "Just about as long as you want me to," I answered. He suggested that I freshen up. Showtime was in one hour!

Showtime was not a problem. I was as ready as I was ever going to be. Just as I finished arranging my western gear on the stage, a young lady came in and told me she was to introduce me. She asked for my resume. Dossier. Well, this certainly was not ranch terminology. I laughed and told her that I had not brought it with me. She said she'd just write down what I told her. I glared at her until she backed off and said to just tell them my name and my occupation.

She introduced me as Hallie Stillwell, ranch woman from Texas. I stepped onto the stage and saw before me a sea of faces. I remembered what Frank Akerman had told me. "Just shoot it to 'em straight from the hip!" And that's what I did. I must have had fair aim, for I spoke for almost two hours, and the students kept me a long time after that with their questions. They were interested in our West Texas rattlesnakes and other varmints. They asked about branding irons. Kentucky ranchers did not brand their cattle. They earmarked them. The students found roundups to be interesting, and they were amazed that we

24

actually burned markings into the skin of our cattle. Most were concerned about the pain that the animals would suffer. I told them that the process was thought not to be terribly painful for we only burned the hair and the outer layer of skin. Some even wanted me to shoot my gun, but I declined saying "Well, I'd like to, but I left my bullets in Texas!" I was pleased with the presentation, and the students seemed to be pleased with what I had to say. The president of the college shook my hand and said, "Mrs. Stillwell, your program is one of the best we have had at this college. Our students were attentive the entire time. I want to thank you." He helped me load my gear into my car and then handed me $150 cash money. I thanked him and put the money into my purse. I drove to the nearest street corner, stopped, and counted the money. I could hardly believe I had earned this much for a two-hour talk. I put $130 into hiding and kept $20 for expenses. I drove away with a smile and the thought that I would have the taxes and the note paid before the banker and tax collector would have time to turn around and blink!

I traveled through Kentucky and spoke at many colleges and auditoriums. I loved what I was doing, but I really missed home. I had started my tour in September and the plan was to be home by Christmas. I almost didn't make it because my schedule was constantly being changed. One president would tell another about my speeches, and before I knew it another stop was added to my itinerary. My last talk was on December 21.

I got to Marathon on December 23 at three in the morning. Immediately I fell into bed fully clothed and slept until ten the next morning. I awoke and drove the rest of the way to the ranch. Home had never been sweeter! Texas soil was beautiful to me even though there still had been no rain. Guy met me at the gate, for he had seen my dust. I had been gone three months and expected a few things to be different, but I was flabbergasted when he blurted out, "Mama, I married Diane while you were gone, and she's gonna live here with us!"

Well, I had known that Guy had sometimes driven up to Alpine to see a girl and had brought her to the ranch a time or two. I felt that this was just a passing fancy, and now this fancy was part of the ranch! I remembered how I had been received as a bride at this ranch, how lonely and left out I had felt when the ranch hands had said that I would never last six months here. I shook off the shock and welcomed Diane to the Stillwell family.

25

I knew that Diane was a city girl who grew up in Alpine. She knew nothing about ranch life. I, too, had once been in her shoes. We would soon find out if she had the right stuff.

Diane wanted to be a good rancher's wife in the worst way. She started at it right away. She cooked our breakfast the first morning and every other morning after that. Guy and I rode out every day, leaving her back at the house. She met us in the evenings with all kinds of questions, about what we did and where we had gone. It seemed as if she was planning something, but I couldn't figure out what.

A couple of weeks later, I awoke as usual to the smell of coffee brewing and bacon frying. This time there was Diane dressed in jeans and a hat. She informed us that she was going with us to work cattle. Guy and I exchanged glances and ate our breakfast in silence. Then we headed for the barn. Guy saddled three horses while I put on my chaps and spurs. Guy handed his wife a pair of chaps, but no spurs. She took about twenty minutes to get them on. Guy and I just stood and watched. When she finished, she declared bravely that she was ready for a good day's work.

She watched me mount up. Guy handed her the reins to her horse, as he climbed into his own saddle. We waited and tried not to look overly concerned. Diane was a large woman, more than six feet tall and large in frame. She studied her horse for a few moments, placed both reins correctly around the horse's neck, and then she grabbed the saddle horn and attempted to throw herself into the saddle. Instead of the saddle, she landed on the other side of the horse. She splattered herself spread-eagle in the dust. It was the funniest thing we had ever seen, though we tried to remain expressionless. She picked herself off the ground and dusted off her clothes. "Zorro and his mother can have all this ranch stuff! I'm sticking to the kitchen!" And she stormed into the house. Guy unsaddled her horse, and we left without a word. Diane never again tried to ride with us, and we never spoke of the incident in her presence.

Diane gave up riding, but she did not give up trying to be a ranch woman. She worked hard, but her efforts sometimes turned into disaster. For example, we had a roadrunner snooping around looking for a hen's nest to rob. I prized my eggs and hated that little devil. I would get my .22-caliber rifle and shoot at him. He was always too quick for me and easily escaped my bullets. Diane watched this contest silently. I was always annoyed when I missed the shot. If you have never shot at a roadrunner, you don't know what a moving target is. The little rascals are almost impossible to hit. One morning Guy and I left early to ride the fences near the black hills. While we were away, the roadrunner came into our yard and Diane spotted him. She ran into the house for a rifle. She took aim, as she had seen me do, and pulled the trigger. It so happened that Guy and I were returning home at this time, and we heard the blast from the gun. The milk calf jumped out of his pen. The horses in the corral bolted and tried to jump the fence. The cows at the water trough stampeded. Guy and I kicked our horses to a gallop and raced to the house. We saw Diane standing near the arbor with a rifle in her hand. She was white as a ghost. Guy demanded to know what happened.

She said, "I was trying to hit that damn roadrunner that Hallie is always shooting at. This gun never sounded like that when she shot it." Guy just shook his head and said, "I guess not. You just shot off a 30.06, not a .22."

I saw her shoulder slump and knew that the rifle had kicked her hard. Guy took the gun and walked in the house, leaving Diane standing there. I unsaddled the horses and fed them and found other work to do in the barn so they could work this out themselves. When I went into the house I didn't say much. I didn't need to.

Things remained calm for several months. Diane stuck to cooking and cleaning the kitchen. She was virtually harmless there. And she was becoming a darn good ranch cook. And even if she wasn't, in the West you never complain about the cooking or you will find yourself doing it.

One day Guy and I mended fences all day. We were coming home just as a heavy shower of rain blew in from the north. We hurried the horses, but soon we realized that we would not be able to cross Maravillas Creek. It was on a big rise. Rain was worth the waiting, considering we had not received any in a long time. We are supposed to get ten inches of rain a year and that day it looked as if we were going to get all of it at once.

While we were waiting on the far side of the Maravillas, Diane heard the roar of water as it poured down the creek bed. The sound is like a Southern Pacific fast freight coming down the tracks. In her panic, Diane ran right up to the cutbank of the creek near the house. Guy and I were on the far side of the canyon and we tried to wave her away from the edge. The roar of water and debris was so great that she could not hear us shouting, "Get back! Get back!"

Suddenly the wall of the creek collapsed and Diane went tumbling down into the torrent. We were horrified. The creek was full of dead trees, big boulders rolling along, and the stream was three-parts gravel to one part water. She was pulled under, rolled over and carried downstream for at least 500 feet before she caught the limb of a big greasewood on the bank. She hung onto the greasewood grimly. Guy and I galloped down the canyon to her, but we were on the wrong side of the torrent and could render no assistance other than to yell encouragement. She couldn't hear that. Finally she was able to pull herself out of the water. These flash floods come and go rather quickly and if you can survive the flash you can survive the ensuing flood. Still, she was covered from head to foot in a tangle of debris, brush, mud, and cactus pads.

Well, this sudden rise turned out to subside not so suddenly. Guy and I were not able to cross for another hour. In the meantime Diane had disappeared. We had no idea what had happened to her, except we felt she was safe from drowning. Still, we were afraid she had been severely injured, perhaps internally. When we were at last able to cross the creek, we raced our horses up to the house and leaped off. We ran around the house searching for her. We found her collapsed on the ground, looking like death warmed over. We got her cleaned up and gave her a cup of coffee and fed her some beans. It turned out that we could see the worst of the damage done to her. She was all scratched up, but her injuries were a long way from the heart. In Texas we consider that which does not kill you makes you stronger. Our Diane had just learned one of the toughest lessons the West has to teach.

Later I started to get the trembles myself. Diane's experience had been a close call! I didn't know anyone else who had survived a flash flood and lived to tell the story. She could easily have drowned and been swept down the Maravillas and into the Rio Grande, and all the way into the Gulf of Mexico, never to be seen again. If Guy and I had been a little delayed we would have known nothing unless we had found her tracks to the creek bank. Then I grew angry. Why, even a fool knows to stay away from a flash flood! From that day on, I worried every time we left the house.

Nevertheless Diane was still a great homemaker, cook, and storyteller. She kept Guy happy and gave us two fine Stillwell boys, Guy Olin (Tige) and Franklin Delmar. She often laughed at herself and told stories about her mishaps to entertain us at family gatherings. We soon accepted the fact that she would never be a real ranch woman. But she was a superb rancher's wife.

Chapter Seven

We struggled through 1950 with little rain. A sprinkle would fall for about ten minutes every month or so. In West Texas a little water goes a long way, but this was far from enough to supply our needs.

Dadie's burdens were becoming ever more heavy. Emeral seldom came to town. Dadie spent most of her days caring for her three little girls and working where she could find work whenever she could. She had finally saved enough money to buy a house in Alpine. We were thankful to have a place to hang our hats in town. I had had to sell the house in Marathon to get money to feed the cows. In all the later years we referred to it as "the house the cows ate." Billie and Everett Wilson bought the house from me, and they lived in it for more than 40 years. Their pleasure in their home was a comfort and joy to me. I always regretted having to sell that house, but I did what had to be done, and looked toward a better future. But you know, Roy had owned that house when we married, and selling it made me feel that a little more of Roy was gone.

Finally life became so difficult for Dadie that I left Guy and Diane in charge of the ranch and moved into Alpine. I knew Diane couldn't ride with Guy. And I knew there were many tasks on the ranch that required more than one hand to do them. But I also knew how badly Dadie needed relief. Once again I was between a rock and a hard place. But I decided to take care of Dadie's girls while she worked. She got a job waiting tables at a café in Alpine. At night Dadie stayed up for hours making western shirts that she sold to local cowboys. By dawn she would be up making breakfast for the girls or giving Nannette a bottle that she frequently had to force down her tiny throat. Nannette just wouldn't take a bottle as a normal infant does.

Dadie knew Nannette was not acting like a normal baby, but no one could really put a finger on the problem. She was not developing as her two older sisters had done. As fall came around the baby's abnormality became ever more obvious. We were all worried, and Dadie decided to search for answers. Our Alpine doctors just weren't finding the problem. I knew that we would have to find a specialist for Nannette. Our local doctor was beginning to agree with us that she was not progressing as she should. Still, he suggested that we wait. And we did!

Guy was having difficulty down on the ranch. For years "wetbacks" drifted across the Stillwell Ranch. I had worked them for years, fed them, and let them sleep in our barn. Often they would be starving, and I would have to feed them for several days before they could do a day's work. I depended on these people. I needed them and they needed me.

President Harry Truman didn't approve of this at all. He determined to have Congress pass a law that would ban the hiring, harboring, or concealing of any alien. This definitely worked a hardship on our ranch.

The Stillwell Ranch is a 22,000-acre spread located on the east side of Big Bend National Park and twenty-five miles north of the Rio Grande. Alien labor was just about the only kind to be had in our sparsely populated area. It was a long drive to the end of the ranch, let alone to where one might go to find any American laborers, even if they could be found. The new labor law provided for a fine of $2,000 and five years in prison. Well, we worked them anyway. The newspapers in the north harped about how ranchers along the Mexican border were exploiting the poor Mexicans, but my treatment of them was never anything but generous. I hired them and worked them as I would any other man. I gave them the opportunity to work at a time when Mexico offered little or nothing. Sometimes I hired men who were passing through, but mostly I hired the same ten or twelve hands whenever we needed help on the ranch.

Well, no one likes to be in violation of the law, so finally I decided that I would naturalize all of my "wet" Mexicans. The immigration officers in the Big Bend were energetic and thorough. Frankly, I thought we would get a whole lot more work done if these men didn't have to dodge the border patrol (*chotas*) all the time. If they were citizens, maybe they would stay with me longer.

I applied for the papers to legalize my men and waited. And waited!

Needless to say, the drouth continued. We know now that the drouth finally broke, but at the time there seemed to be no end in sight. I needed to feed cattle, but I knew I could borrow no more at the bank. Even so, I drove to Alpine one more time just to feel out the banker about a few additional dollars on my loan. When I arrived at the bank, it was closed. This was a weekday. Down in the Big Bend we often lose track of time, but this was no holiday I could think of. I met a friend on the street who told me that the bank was closed because the cashier had committed suicide. Supposedly he had been embezzling money. Well, when it doesn't rain, it doesn't pour! More than likely the bank would have to call its loans. I had the collateral to pay off the notes, but I would lose nearly everything.

My head was spinning as I drove the road east to Marathon, and then south back to the ranch. Suddenly, like a light bulb coming on, I got an idea! Wax. We were then in the Korean War, and there was a new demand for candelilla wax. I might have plenty of troubles, but I also had plenty of candelilla. Candelilla is wax plant. On the ranch it grows in great abundance in the worst kind of places—places where nothing else will grow. It is a gray little plant with no leaves, just stems, and unless you knew better you might think it was dead. You might also think it was a worthless desert plant, but the stems are coated with a layer of wax, which helps the plant retain its moisture. Son had made money from candelilla a number of years before. I decided to put up another wax factory. I would do it right away.

Guy was not much interested in my wax scheme, so I hired a Mexican foreman and he did the rest. We bought two *pilos* (vats). Unfortunately wax processing requires a lot of water, but we still had water in our wells, so we got started. We bought acid, burros, packsaddles, and ropes. Even so, the start-up cost for me was less than $150. We were in operation within a week. The first month I made $600. I split that with the foreman. Within four months we were clearing over $1,000 a month. Believe me, this money pulled us out of a real mess. It turned out that the bank did not call my note, but they did freeze all lending. With the wax operation, though, we had enough cash to run the ranch.

Just when things were really rolling, our well at the wax camp dried up. I couldn't afford to haul water way out there. Guy suggested we hire a water witcher. He was being funny. Guy was a successful water witcher and had often found water on the ranch. I took him out to the wax camp. He walked around for about thirty minutes and then pointed to a spot. I instructed our Mexican man to dig there. He dug down about twenty feet, and we had a new source of water. We were back in business!

Our wax business enabled me to make a large payment on our bank note. One day I noticed that some of the men who were packing bags of wax were dropping them into a mud pit. Of course this caused them to weigh more. This meant I was paying for both wax and mud, since I was paying the men by the total weight of the wax processed. I began to check each bag as it was loaded. Some men had even put rocks in the bags. Roy had often told me to pay close attention to the details. From that time on, I kept a closer eye on the workers.

All this time we were producing wax, I was waiting for the government to process the paperwork on my fifteen "wet" Mexicans. Many of my Big Bend neighbors had received clearance on their hands. I called the authorities in El Paso and got nothing but excuses. I figured the squeaky wheel gets oil, and I kept after them. Finally they got tired of my complaints. They notified me to take my men to Eagle Pass. I was given specific guidelines for transporting my men. Each man must have a seat. There must be a fire extinguisher, a first aid kit, and a shelter over their heads. I would have to convert our truck into a bus. When I told the Mexicans what had to be done, they got right to work and had the truck ready in two days. We were on our way.

We followed the road east, which runs along the Southern Pacific railroad tracks. At one point a freight train roared past us, causing panic among the men. Many of them came from small villages in rural Mexico. They had never seen a train. They tore off the canvas shelter and jumped out of the truck! I had had plenty of experience rounding up cattle, but this was the first time I had to round up Mexicans!

In Langtry, Judge Roy Bean's old town, we had to check the men in with the Immigration Office. Each man was required to provide his name, age, birth date, and birthplace. Most of them were scared to death. Some waited outside as if they were ready to run at the first sign. Most of them had never been more than twenty miles from their village. They were accustomed to running at the sight of immigration officers. Now they were expected to give them personal information. They were terrified it might be used against them. The officials had little patience and were quite rude, which was not helpful. The men gave the shortest possible answers to the questions they were being asked. This interrogation went on and on. All the paperwork had to be filled out. It seemed to me that the officials were making it as hard as possible for these men to become naturalized citizens. They may have thought they could intimidate us into just going back to Mexico. They had never dealt with Hallie Stillwell!

After four hours of paperwork, we were back on the road and headed for Eagle Pass. We stopped in Del Rio to spend the night. I took a room in the hotel. The men camped out wherever they could find a spot. We were back on the road at dawn. I stopped at a grocery store to purchase our breakfast, which consisted of two loaves of bread, bologna, and milk. We ate quickly in a grove of cottonwoods and continued on our way to the immigration office in Eagle Pass. When we got there, we found the Mexican government had shut down all processing the day before. When I saw the dismay on the men's faces, I muscled my way through the crowd to the official in charge. I told him our plight. He said that nothing could be done. He turned and left me standing in my tracks. For this we pay taxes. We got back in the truck and returned to the ranch.

I got little labor from the men the week after we returned from Eagle Pass, so I let them take a holiday while I drove up to Marathon to get the mail. At the post office I had a letter notifying me that Mexico and the U. S. had settled their disagreement and the processing center in Eagle Pass was open again. They issued another date for me to appear with my hands.

So off we went again. By the time we got to Sanderson, the men had become festive. They were singing and clapping their hands. My spirits lifted. Surely this time we would be successful. Two of the men rode in the cab with me. The rest were in the back. The man beside me dropped his head and began snoring. I saw the bottle of whiskey under his shirt. I was furious. I couldn't process a drunken Mexican. I pulled the bottle out. My first inclination was to empty the contents out the window as I drove along. But I decided not to make an issue of the matter. When we reached Dryden we stopped for a rest. The drunk Mexican woke up and began a search for his bottle. I gave him a stern talk. Then I lectured the rest of them. The contrite culprit went into a restaurant and bought me a cup of coffee. When we arrived in Langtry, he jumped from the truck and doused himself in a water trough. I made him go last in the line at the immigration office. He passed the test. Boy, was I relieved! Then we were on the road again.

When we arrived in Eagle Pass, we encountered more stumbling blocks. I signed some papers. Then they sent me to another office where I was required to sign an affidavit swearing that I would work no more illegal aliens. Next we were sent to the International Bridge between Eagle Pass and Piedras Negras. We had to park the truck about four blocks away and walk to the bridge. I must have looked like a *comandante* with my ragged little army.

Well, we waited at least four hours at the American end of the bridge awaiting instructions. Finally we were directed to cross the bridge into Mexico to get the men's citizenship cards stamped. The older men encountered no difficulty but the men between the ages of eighteen and twenty-six were being held because they were eligible for the army. By this time I was at the end of my patience. I stormed into the office, on the Mexican side of course, and illegally! They escorted me back across the river to *el otro lado* (the other side). I was really steamed! Though the officers were not willing to talk with me, it turned out they were willing to talk with my foreman—on their side of the river—so he went back across the bridge to Mexico. All I could think was "What if they keep him?" I could not run the wax camp without him. I had to get him back. Two hours passed, and he returned with two soldiers.

He told me the situation could be fixed if I paid $10 for each man. The Mexican government would forget that they needed my men for the army. Well, this was not my first trip to the rug market. I told my foreman to go back and negotiate some more. He gave me a little smile, and back he went.

Two hours later he returned again. He had talked the officials down to about half of their original demand. I paid them off. While all this was going on, I discovered that my men had disappeared.

The U.S. officials told me to get all my men together. The older men had disappeared, and the younger ones had not yet returned from Mexico. What to do? I had to wait for those coming from the Mexican side, so I sent my foreman out to look for the older group. Soon the younger men appeared, but the older men were still missing. My foremen found the missing men in a cantina and they were drunk! Nevertheless I took them to the American officials for their final processing. They had physical examinations and were issued their identity cards. By this time it was nearly dark and I was exhausted, so I got a hotel room. The men slept in the truck. The next morning we ate a quick breakfast of honey and bread and started our long trip home. The first thing they wanted to do was stop in Del Rio, so they could legally shop in the American stores. I dropped them off in downtown Del Rio, while I retreated to a restaurant and got myself a cool drink. I rested there for two hours and when I returned to pick the men up downtown, no one was there. I waited until sundown and still no men. I went back to the restaurant and ate supper. Since the men had still not returned, I checked into a hotel. I hoped they would spot the truck parked outside.

The next morning I went across the river to Villa Acuña, Del Rio's companion city. I went to the jail and sure enough, all my men were locked up. They had been arrested for drunk and disorderly conduct. The police officer was quite cordial. The men were American citizens now. He could not figure out why they had come over to Mexico to get drunk, but I would have to pay their fines. I asked "How much?" "Dos pesos," he replied with a smile.

I paid up and marched my men back to the other side. Not one of them said a word or even looked at me. I was mad enough to bite a rattlesnake. When we were finally on the road again, I asked my foreman why they went to Mexico after they had just been made American citizens. He said they wanted to see if their cards worked! I just shook my head in amazement. These men had dragged me through the keyhole. The whole thing had cost me at least $700. But we were all legal. Roy's "truth policy" has always kept me out of trouble. I have often thanked him for that. He said that honesty paid more than it cost, but this latest episode seemed to disprove his theory. Even so, I had done the right thing, and though forty years has passed since that time, I would not do it any differently now.

Chapter Eight

Our *braceros* settled back to work after our long ordeal. They kept us alive with the wax camp. I have always been grateful for their loyalty and willingness to work so hard. Often I think about how many times Mexican workers have come to the aid of the Stillwell Ranch. They are really good people.

In September Son wrote that he was ready to come home. He found a man who wanted to purchase the Oregon ranch. I made reservations to take the train out there. I would stop in Colorado and visit the Bensons, then continue to Oregon.

I was pleased to see that our scrawny cattle had filled out. They were beautiful, fat, smooth, and muscular. I hadn't seen such fine cattle in a long time. The grass was as tall as the calves. I marveled at the beauty of the land. I wondered if we should move the entire family to Oregon and sell the Big Bend ranch. Though that idea was tempting, I knew we were Texas born and Texas bred, and that when it came time to die, we would be buried in Texas.

Son's cabin consisted of one room with a fireplace, a wood cookstove, a small counter, and a table with two chairs. The room had two small windows and a huge wooden door. As we sat there and drank our coffee, I could see why Son was ready to come home. This place was beautiful, but it simply wasn't the Big Bend.

We went over to see the man who wanted to buy the ranch. He was willing to pay more than either of us expected, so I agreed to sell. We had made money on the deal, paid all of our expenses, and then some. We decided to sell most of our cattle in Oregon rather than ship them back to Texas, which was still in the grip of the drouthy fifties. We kept only the pick of the herd and all of our bulls.

We shipped the cattle and drove back to Texas in Son's truck. We took turns driving, and in only three days we were back in Texas. We crossed the Guadalupe Mountains near El Paso and then came through the Davis Mountains. "These are the bluest mountains I have ever seen," Son commented. "I know why Dad picked the Big Bend for his ranch. It's the best place on earth!"

Once back in Alpine, we went straight to Dadie's because I was worried about Nannette. We had a family counsel. The ranch could not provide for all of us anymore. Son agreed that he would seek work somewhere in the area. He accepted the fact that he could not return to the ranch for a living.

I stayed in Alpine with Dadie. Son began a search for employment. Within a week he found some farmland near Presidio, and he and Emeral decided to go together and purchase a D-6 Catapillar. Son would lease the Presidio property for farming. Son would farm and get prospects for the tractor. Emeral would drive the tractor.

Shortly after Son returned from Oregon, he began to court Gwin Kring Roberts, a woman he had known before leaving. She had been married previously and had two children, Brenda and Scotty. Son and Gwin were married one month later. She and the children moved to Presidio with Son. In Presidio Gwin opened a small store while Son farmed his land and built irrigation ditches for area farmers. Son drove the tractor when Emeral wasn't around, which made for twelve- to fourteen-hour days. But they managed to feed their family.

The 1950s drouth was the longest that ranchers in West Texas had ever experienced. Nevertheless we were stayers, not quitters. And if we had little else, we had faith in the future.

Chapter Nine

The ranch continued to lose ground in 1952 and 1953. Now Guy was working odd jobs to help feed himself, Diane, and their new son Tige. Basically the cattle were fending for themselves except when a wax check would provide enough cash to buy cattle feed. Dadie gave birth to a fourth girl, Marlene. Two months after she was born, Dadie collapsed in the kitchen one morning. She was alone with the four girls, and she couldn't walk or talk. She managed to tell Kay, the eldest, with sign language that she must go for help. Kay ran to the neighbors. By the time I got there, the neighbor had Dadie sitting up, but she still couldn't speak. We loaded her into my car, and I rushed her to Fort Stockton to a doctor who was trained in more advanced medicine than those in Alpine. After a thorough examination, he concluded that she was suffering from exhaustion. It was obvious to me that Dadie could no longer carry all the weight of raising her family. Nannette's palsy, another baby to feed, and all the bills to pay were at least temporarily beyond her abilities. The doctor told us that Dadie must have at least six weeks of total bed rest.

Dadie in bed for even two days would be difficult on all of us, much less six weeks! Dadie was a pillar of stone in our lives. In all her life, she was never known to shirk a task. She never asked for help, though she would sometimes accept it.

Our friends helped take care of the three older girls. Dadie was still breast-feeding Marlene, who frequently cried and fussed and would stay with no one but Dadie or me. I was then working in a flower shop in Alpine, so desperate were the times. But I took time off to stay at home with Dadie. I cared for her and Marlene night and day. Gwin and Diane helped with the other girls.

After two weeks Dadie had recovered enough to be able to walk about a bit, and while she had been in bed, she had come to a major decision. She had earned a degree from Our Lady of the Lake in San Antonio, which qualified her to teach. And that was what she was going to do! We decided that I would keep Marlene, and she would take the other three girls where she could find employment. She took the first teaching job she was offered in Tornillo, Texas, a remote town near El Paso.

We moved Dadie and the three older girls to Tornillo in late August of 1953. Son drove a truck loaded with her belongings and we followed in the car. We drove all day and got into Tornillo around dusk. This is a long trip even by today's standards, but back then the roads were not as good, and of course automobiles were not nearly so reliable. I recall that trip with trepidation. I felt my heart was being ripped out with my daughter moving so far away. I would not be able to see her or my grandchildren for long periods of time, perhaps only at Christmas or Easter.

We were all up at dawn the next day. That was one beautiful sunrise. It seemed to tell me that finally, at last, our deliverance was at hand. We drove to the school where Dadie had been provided a teacherage. This is a quaint concept today, but fifty years ago in rural Texas, teachers were often provided with a house beside the school as part of their salary. The house was called a teacherage. We got Dadie all set up in her new house, and by noon Son and I waved goodbye to Dadie and her girls and left them standing on the front step of her new home. The girls were all weeping, and I suppose so were Dadie and I. Though we were confident now in the future, it is always difficult to rip children out of their familiar world and transplant them onto strange soil. Even so, I knew those little girls were tough. They were Stillwells.

So Dadie's career as a teacher began. The teaching went well, but her girls were often unaccountably sick. The bottom line was that Dadie could not continue teaching and care for them, so they returned to Alpine in November. Kay, Linda, and Nannette moved back into my house in Alpine. All of them had measles. We lived through the measles epidemic. Christmas came. Dadie came to Alpine to visit during the school holiday, and we regrouped.

At the ranch all the surface water tanks had dried up by the beginning of 1954. Guy drove up to Alpine to tell me in person that the water well at the house had dried up. That well was our lifeline. We had no other source of water but the Rio Grande, twenty-five miles away, and even the river had dried up, flowing only a little deep in its sands. Marathon, being higher in elevation and closer to the mountains, still had a few sources of water. So drinking water was brought from town in jugs. Taking a bath was simply out of the question. Dishes and eating utensils were cleaned with sand.

I asked Guy if he remembered the time Luther Yarbro had come to the ranch and witched our land for a well. Luther was supposed to be one of the best witchers in Texas. Guy remembered the spot that Luther had recommended. He said it was too sandy and not a likely place for a well. Nevertheless I insisted we try there.

I loaded up my grandchildren and off we went. We moved back to the ranch. I was going to find water there or die trying. During the day Diane took care of all six children, Dadie's four girls and her own two lively boys. Guy and I started searching for water. We had to do it on the cheap, because I couldn't borrow any more money at the bank.

We could not afford to take any of my now naturalized Mexican workmen away from the wax camp, so we hired some "wet" Mexicans, who continued to stream across our land.

I told Diane that I would take the girls back to Alpine and wait until we could get some men to dig the new well. Four Mexicans came up to the ranch looking for work a few days later. Guy sent word to Alpine that we were ready to begin. Within an hour of getting his message, I took the girls and headed for the ranch. I told Guy to have the Mexicans use our Fresno to clear away the sand before the digging began. A Fresno is a piece of machinery used for clearing away sand, mud, and gravel. Mules usually pulled the machine at that time, but we were fortunate to have one that was motorized. Guy and I showed them the spot where we were going to dig. We gave them instructions, especially about watching for the *chotas*, and we left to do other chores.

Shortly after the first day of digging began, the four men showed up at the house and told us that they were sick and were going back to Mexico. We gave them a half-day's pay and they left. Guy and I went out to the well site where we cleared the spot with the Fresno. This took days of work. We decided to wait to see if any more Mexicans came through who would be willing to dig the well. A few days later three more Mexicans came through looking for work. Times may have been tough in Texas, but in Mexico things were worse.

Immediately Guy put the men to digging. I was so anxious about the water well that I sat on a sand dune every day and watched as the men dug. I felt that if I stayed there on the site, the men wouldn't leave. Either Guy or I always stayed on guard duty looking for the *chotas*, so we could warn the men whenever we saw anyone. With the drouth on for so many years, we could always tell if a vehicle was coming by the trail of dust it left behind. Most of the time we could see or hear horseback riders long before they got to the ranch. Diane also had a cocker spaniel that warned us of visitors, whether man or beast.

One day Guy and I had to ride down Maravillas Canyon to look for some missing cattle. We didn't leave anyone guarding. Sure enough, the *chotas* sneaked up on the workers. They couldn't run because they were down in the well hole.

As Guy and I rode into the house trap, we saw our men being tied up by the border patrolmen. I jumped from the horse and begged and pleaded for the men to be left alone just until we hit water. I persisted to no avail. They loaded the men into the back of their truck.

I walked up to the officer in charge and glared at him. "Just you don't go and take them too far up river to cross back into Mexico, because it will take them too long to get back!" Our digging stopped, but those same three men showed up in the middle of the night two days later. Soon we were all back at the well site.

Several days after they returned, our neighbor Delmar Collins came to the ranch. He climbed out of his truck and walked to where I was sitting. He asked, "What in the world are you doing, Hallie?"

"I'm digging a well, and I'm going to have water before you know it." I answered. "Well, the drouth has gotten to your brain, Hallie," he replied, "that is no place to dig a well." Of course Guy agreed with Del as he chimed in, "I've already told her that."

I responded that I had learned a few things from living in the Big Bend and that Luther Yarbro had marked this spot for a good well, and that Luther was one of the best witchers in the country. If we didn't find water in this well, Guy would have to move to town. With no one at the ranch, I felt that there would be no chance we could save Roy's dream.

Guy came home from town one day and told me he had heard at the post office how crazy I was. There wasn't a soul in Marathon who believed I would find water in a sand pile. I was sure Guy agreed with them. Nevertheless our men continued to dig. About ten days after the digging started one of the men came to the house and wanted us to follow him to the well site. We dropped what we were doing and rushed over there.

One of the men handed me a handful of damp sand. Well, damp sand does not make a well, but I told the men to keep digging. By then the well was deep enough that the men were having difficulty getting in and out of the hole. It was taking a long time to drag the buckets of dirt from the bottom to the top of the hole to be emptied. The Mexicans told Guy they needed some long rope and a pulley. We got them what they asked for. They made a windlass, a device used for many years to take dirt and rocks out of wells. After this the digging went much faster.

Five days after they found the damp sand, one of the Mexicans struck his pick into the bottom and suddenly water flowed rapidly into the well. I was in the house cooking dinner when I heard all the shouting. As I stepped out onto the porch, one of the Mexicans ran right into me. He grabbed my arm and we ran over to the well. There was nothing to be seen in the bottom of the hole but water. Wonderful, beautiful, glorious water! I couldn't quit looking at it.

The men dug down twenty feet and stuck solid rock. Water was still flowing into the well, but we had not hit the vein. We needed some dynamite to crack that rock ledge, but I knew we couldn't obtain it in Marathon. I told the men to keep hammering at that rock. I had a look in my eye that told them they had better do it, too. They assaulted that ledge two weeks with their pick-axes and finally got through the rock layer. They still had not hit the aquifer. Grimly I ordered them to keep digging.

On the sixty-fourth day we hit real water. The hole filled up and stayed full. This new well provided the house and stock with plenty of water. Today, more than forty years later, our well is still a good one. Had we not struck water in that well, we would have sold all our stock and moved to town. But one more time the ranch was saved. To this very day I still have faith in water witchers.

Chapter Ten

The elation we felt upon finding a new source of water was short-lived. Guy began to suffer chronic aches and pains throughout his body. He never could quite figure out what was causing it. Often he would wake up and be unable to move. It might take him an hour to get out of bed. His back ached and his legs were numb.

I drove Guy to Alpine to see Dr. Hill. Dr. Hill examined Guy carefully, but he could not determine what was wrong. He told Guy to rest and take pain pills. He felt that perhaps the cause was a strained muscle in his back or leg. We left, no better off than before the visit. Guy took a pain pill and slept most of the way back to the ranch.

Once we got to Marathon, I stopped and picked up the mail. I had a few bills and a letter from Virginia in New York. I had been so overwhelmed with ranch and family problems that I had given little thought to our book. Almost six months had passed since I had done any research on it.

Virginia was pressing me to come to New York so we could work together on the book. I hardly had time to answer her letters much less make another trip to New York. There was no way I could take time off from my responsibilities at home.

Guy could not work at all. All he could do was lie in bed or sit around the house. When he was no better after two months, I took him back to Dr. Hill. Another examination revealed nothing new. Dr. Hill referred us to a specialist in El Paso. So off to El Paso we went. The doctor there diagnosed Guy with a herniated disk. The fifth vertebrae had slipped completely out of place. Armed with this information, we went back to the ranch to await further developments.

Two weeks later we got a letter summoning us to Dr. Hill's office. That was it! No explanations. We left early the next day. He told us that surgery was the only alternative. He recommended the Mayo Clinic.

He might as well have recommended the Taj Mahal. The Mayo Clinic was so far beyond our means as to be unattainable. We had no medical insurance whatsoever. We were deeply in debt to the bank, and our only source of income was the candelilla wax camp. I told the doctor that some other arrangements would have to be made.

Dr. Hill thought for a few moments for the second best alternative. Finally he said that there was a surgeon in El Paso who could do the job. He said he would call the doctor and let us know when or if we should drive over there.

The next day Dr. Hill called to tell us to go to the hospital in El Paso. Dadie took over the family. She and Gwin would take care of the babies while Diane and I took Guy to El Paso.

The surgery was scheduled and took place. It seemed to relieve some of Guy's pain. But the doctor told us that Guy could never ride a horse again. He could do no lifting, no more manual labor. He said that if Guy violated these instructions, future surgery could never repair the damage. Guy returned to the ranch, but life had changed. Dadie was home for the summer and had the care of the girls. But Guy had few things to keep him busy. It was six months before he would walk normally again.

By this time Dadie had filed for divorce from Emeral. She returned to Alpine and worked during the summer. She hired a girl from Ojinaga, across the river from Presidio, to live with her and take care of the girls. This left me free to stay with Guy and Diane and keep the ranch running as best we could. Diane kept the house, fed us all, and did everything for Guy. I was left to run the ranch. I had been back only three weeks when I realized our cattle at Black Gap were going to die of thirst. We would have to move the cattle from Black Gap to Maravillas. And I was the only one left in the family who could ride. Guy and I spent several evenings planning the move.

The next morning our Mexican foreman and I saddled up and set out for Black Gap. As we rode off, I looked back at Guy, standing at the gate with a sad look on his face. I knew he was feeling terrible because his poor old mom was back to doing the man's work again.

The two of us rounded up the cattle and that night we made camp, so we could be ready to move the herd at dawn. As I laid my bedroll down, I thought back to the winter Roy and I spent moving cattle from the ranch to Marathon for shipping. Roy had lit an old dead sotol bush for our campfire to make me comfortable. That one simple event was what Roy was all about. He never expressed himself much in words. You knew him by his actions. I dozed off to sleep under the stars and moon with memories I will cherish as long as I live.

The next day we arose before dawn. After a breakfast of biscuits and coffee, we saddled our horses and prepared to move the cattle. The drive took all day. We got to the Maravillas as the sun was sinking in the west.

We rode into the house trap about an hour after dusk. We unsaddled in the dark. Diane warmed our supper. I just dropped into a chair and started eating. Then I slept until ten o'clock the next morning.

For weeks I watched Guy sit and mope. I was rather alarmed to hear him refer to the Stillwell Ranch as "this god-forsaken place." Forsaken it undoubtedly was, but not by God, whose Plan was beyond our knowledge. I decided to send Guy off on a trip. Anything to distract him until he could gain some strength in his back. I insisted Diane should go with him. There was no money for a real vacation, so they decided they would visit Diane's parents in Alpine.

I continued running the ranch with our Mexican foreman. Son came occasionally from Presidio to help. In addition to our many new troubles, the old customary drouth continued unabated.

I heard that a man in Alpine was interested in purchasing the Stillwell Ranch. I invited him to come down and look the place over. He did so one day and then went back to Alpine. I spent a very restless night weighing the different alternatives. The next day I drove up to Alpine to talk to my banker. He told me the price I would have to get to pay all my debts. It was certain I would get that much for the place, but if we were going to give it up, we would have to have quite a bit more than that in order for us to live. I doubted if I could get that much. When I returned to the ranch, I looked over the mountains and smelled the greasewood. I sat in the arbor Roy and I had made. After a long time brooding over it, I decided to sell the ranch. There just wasn't enough to hold it together. I talked about it with my friend Willie Henderson. He told me I could pasture my herd on some of his land close to Alpine. Alpine was much higher in elevation than the Stillwell Ranch, so it received more rain and had better grass. I still had about eighty head left. So when I sold the ranch, at least we would have a place to put the cattle. Son had recently taken a load of cows to San Angelo to sell. They had brought eleven cents on the hoof, not good, so it was pointless for us to sell our cattle at that time.

I knew that when I sold the ranch, Roy's dream would die. Yet, I didn't feel I could force any more problems on my family. Nor could I expect the bank to continue backing me.

I returned to Alpine and went to see Mae Ament, a longtime friend who was also a lawyer. Mae told me what I would have to do to sell the ranch. I telephoned the buyer and told him I had made the decision to sell. He made a reasonable offer but he said he would need time to get some cash together. He said he would get back to me in a few weeks.

I was dreadfully depressed for three days. I couldn't bear the thought of selling the ranch. I went to town to talk with Dick Rogers, the president of the bank. I said, "Dick, I want to keep the ranch. I know I should sell, but my heart is just not in it. What can I do?"

Dick looked at me and shook his head. He had always supported me in every way, but I knew I was out of rope. He settled back in his big office chair and said, "Hallie, I can help you feed your cattle, but I can't feed your family. You will have to do that. I don't know how you can do it, but that's as much as our bank can do for you. I wish I could help more, but I can't!"

I left the bank knowing Dick had gone beyond what most any other banker would do. Even so, I would not sell. I would keep the ranch!

I called the family together and told them where we stood. Son said he was sure he could find work for his tractor. During the summer Dadie had begun looking for a teaching job closer to home. She found one in Grandfalls on the Pecos River north of Fort Stockton. She would be able to take the girls with her. That would free me to do the ranching. Guy said he could get a job at Big Bend National Park. Diane would be looking for a teaching job. She hoped to be hired for the school in the park. Guy and Diane would live at the ranch and tend the stock. I would have to keep the ranch going and find a way to pay the taxes.

Sis Benson was having problems of her own. Gene, her husband, had diabetes. He would have to have a leg amputated. She asked me to work more hours in the flower shop. As an incentive she offered me her garage apartment. I accepted her offer and moved out of Dadie's house in Alpine. Dadie's teaching position in Grandfalls included a teacherage, so she was able to rent her house for additional income.

One day I was having lunch with Mae Ament in Alpine. She mentioned that she was trying to find a guardian for five Mexican children. Their parents were both dead, but there was an insurance policy of $10,000 to provide for them. She said she had been unable to find someone to administer this fund.

I asked her if it paid anything. She said "A little."

"I'll do it!" I exclaimed. She stared at me for a moment as though she was questioning what to say and then simply answered, "You've got it."

Things were not getting any better, but now they were not getting any worse. We managed to pay the taxes and feed the cattle. But we sure were not living very well. We were still a family. We still had the ranch. The pleasure I got from that and seeing my children and grandchildren still made it all worthwhile.

Gene Benson was a cattle buyer and he often attended cattle sales. But he could no longer go alone after the amputation of his leg. I became his traveling companion and driver. We attended auctions and cattle sales all over West Texas. I enjoyed this very much. I had many opportunities to speak with people who were having the same problems as we were. Gradually I came to understand that the Stillwells were not the only folks living in difficult times.

After I had spent a year in the Benson garage apartment, Sis and Gene offered me a room in their home. I was glad to accept since the apartment had no kitchen or bath facilities. I had only a coffeepot and a small hot plate. Moving into their home gave me some appreciated creature comforts. The Benson family had helped me out more times than I could count.

One morning I was in the Holland Hotel having a cup of coffee when I struck up a conversation with a reporter for the *El Paso Times*. We chatted for an hour about the drouth, the hard times, ranch life, I forget what all. He asked if I would be interested in becoming a correspondent for the *Times*. Of course I agreed at once.

With three different jobs, now I felt better. As I look back on those hard times, I would not want to repeat them, but they certainly made us all stronger people. Of course, without family and friends we never would have been able to get through it and hold on to the ranch. I am now ninety-nine years of age. It has been nearly fifty years since my husband Roy passed away, leaving the legacy of the Stillwell Ranch in my hands. All these years I have been aware of Roy's presence, standing right behind me many times. Hard times were also our legacy, but with Roy's teaching, we did it. I am deeply proud to have been able to tell you all about it.

Soon it will pass to the hands of my children and their children. And a new chapter in the history of the Stillwell Ranch will be written.

After completing this manuscript, Hallie Stillwell passed away on August 18, 1997, two months and two days short of her 100th birthday.

HALLIE'S PHOTOS

Caption on photograph reads: "Private school — San Angelo. Hallie 5th from left Top children.
Mabel [Hallie's sister] 1st on right first standing row." This photo was probably taken around 1905 when Hallie lived in San Angelo.

Hallie with Roy and Son around 1948 at the old home place.

Dadie Stillwell, 1939.

Guy Stillwell,
about 1948.

Dadie Stillwell
and Betty
Barber Heath at
Hallie's house
in Marathon.

Hallie with a Mexican water witcher.

Hallie with some of the ranch hands.

53

Guy Stillwell and son, Tige, overlooking the Stillwell Ranch in an undated photograph.

Dadie's graduation picture, 1942, from Our Lady of the Lake.

Diane Pierce Stillwell, 1959

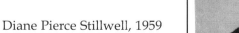

Emily Kay, 1959

Nanette, age 9,
1958

Linda, age 10, 1958

Marlene, age 6,
1958

Travis, age 3, 1958

Hallie's Grandchildren

Guy "Tige," 1959

Franklin "Frank,"
1960

Hallie Stillwell. Stan's Alpine Studio, March 1968.

Hallie and Governor John Connally, March 28, 1968, at the opening of Guadalupe Mountains National Park.

Hallie and World Champion Chili Master H. Allen Smith (Soupy to his friends).

23rd ANNUAL
ORIGINAL
TERLINGUA INTERNATIONAL
FRANK X. TOLBERT — WICK FOWLER MEMORIAL
CHAMPIONSHIP CHILI COOK-OFF

NOVEMBER 4, 1989
BEHIND THE STORE at VIVA TERLINGUA

Music by GARY P. NUNN — WAYNE KENNEMER
and the "National Band of Texas"

WOLF CHILI

SPONSORS: WOLF BRAND CHILI • TOLBERT'S CHILI PARLOR
WICK FOWLER'S 2-ALARM CHILI • LONE STAR BEER
SHINER BREWERY • COLONY PARKE HOTEL/DALLAS

Hallie the Chili Queen at the 1989 Terlingua Festival. Kathleen Tolbert Ryan (Frank X. Tolbert's daughter) stands on Hallie's right. Malcolm Fox is the master of ceremonies.

Hallie (seated) with her longtime friend and co-author Virginia Madison.

Hallie holding a copy of the first volume of her memoirs, *I'll Gather My Geese*, published in 1991. She is sitting in front of the just-completed Hallie Stillwell Hall of Fame.

Dadie and Hallie on the Stillwell Ranch, June 1987.

Guy Stillwell in
Maravillas Canyon
in 1991.

Dadie and Hallie at the counter of the Stillwell Store. The store not only served the many tourists who passed through the Big Bend, but also the local ranchers, who were in the habit of landing their airplane on the road outside the store.

Judge Hallie Stillwell has just married Steven Stetten and Mary Beth Lee at the Gage Hotel in Marathon, December 11, 1993.

HALLIE THE STORYTELLER

Hallie Stillwell was a storyteller and she liked to write. She wrote of many things in her beloved Big Bend—people, places, and events. She was a part-time reporter for several newspapers, but her most faithful contributions were to the *Alpine Avalanche*. As Ranching News editor, she kept folks informed on what was going on out in the hinterlands. The hinterlands extended to wherever Hallie went. Sometimes they got as far as New York City.

Only two of the following stories appeared in print, "Why Wyoming" was in the *Alpine Avalanche* on August 24, 1956, and "Bottle of Wine" was published in the *El Paso Times* in 1963. The other stories were written throughout her life. She kept them in her files, which is where Betty Heath found them.

Why Wyoming

I am writing from Laramie, Wyoming, a college town, with an altitude of over 7,000 feet. For a distance of about seventy-five miles before arriving, we hit clouds and fog so dense that vision was cut to zero. But we crept along, climbing, climbing and wondering just how high we would go. With the radio playing beautiful organ selections for Sunday morning worship and the narrow road obscured by earthbound clouds, I felt for sure I was headed for the Land of Eternity. All of a sudden we were above the clouds and there was Laramie.

I feel at home in Wyoming with friends Mary and Buddy Gibbs. For the present they are located here with Continental Oil Company. They are from San Angelo, and Mary is a sister to Virginia Madison with whom I am making this trip, along with Dick and Dolly Madison.

Wyoming is a lot like Texas — cattle, sheep, oil, tourists, and drouth. Today Wyoming is one of the nation's leading producers of petroleum with its refineries, pipe lines, and other related industries. Oil has become one of Wyoming's leading industrial operations.

The high open ranges of Wyoming mountains afford ideal grazing grounds for millions of sheep, with many of the sheep ranches still using sheep-herders. Cowboys still brand calves on the open range of huge cattle ranches.

It was the Texas cattlemen who initiated drives to the north searching for new markets and open range for their herds of Longhorns. With his lariat, bull[whip], hide chaps, high heel boots, ten-gallon hat, six-shooter, and cowpony, the cowboy took his place in our American heritage.

With high mountains — some reaching over 12,000 feet — providing wonderful summer range and the valleys giving good winter range, the Wyoming sheep industry remains one of the top wool producers in the United States.

How valuable the tourist industry is to Wyoming is illustrated by the fact that it ranks third in importance behind agriculture and oil in the state today.

We left Alpine August 16 for New York City via Wyoming. The Davis Mountains were green since the recent spotted rains, but the grass is still short. We didn't see any cattle or sheep to mention until we reached the Roswell, New Mexico, area. On the fields through here we saw some, and they looked good. The mountains near Albuquerque and Santa Fe were green and stock looked good.

At Las Vegas, New Mexico, we stopped to see my cousins Tommie and Ida Sowell who ranch on a large spread about thirty miles from the Pecos River. They came to this Las Vegas area ten years ago from Sterling City, Texas, and they have never regretted the move. They have held on in spite of drouth and done well. Their cattle are fat, and there is no feeding around here. However, the rains are spotted like in the Big Bend country. There is some activity here in cattle buying with prices on calves about seventeen cents to twenty cents.

Bottle of Wine

The Stillwell Ranch in the Big Bend Country lies forty-six miles southeast of Marathon and is known to have been the location of a large Indian campground. Many artifacts remain there just as the Indians left them. Shelters in the bluffs of the Maravillas shut-up and other canyons house cracked-up rocks lying in soot several feet deep. One finds rock paintings, morteros, and metates, along with hundreds of rock mounds where fires were kept burning. All these relics tell the story of the many Indians who camped here for a long period of time.

History tells us that many Roman Catholic monks and priests came into this area to convert the Indians and to search for gold and other precious metals. The "Seven Cities of Gold" that Coronado reported to the King of Spain was still very much in their thoughts. But little, if any, physical evidence has ever been found to prove that the monks and priests actually visited in the Indian campgrounds, until recently.

Just a few weeks ago, Guy Stillwell stepped out of his kitchen door and sauntered up on a sand dune near the ranch to take a look-see up the road leading out of the ranch. He stumped his toe on a small object sticking up out of the sand. Turning around, he gave it a little kick. The object didn't budge! Curious as to the size of what he couldn't see, he started digging. To his amazement a huge bottle began to emerge from the sand. He had never seen such a bottle!

In perfect condition, dark green in color, with a capacity of about five gallons, the vessel was made of a kind of glass unfamiliar to Guy. His curiosity was greatly aroused. He took the bottle into Alpine and put it in a downtown shop window hoping that someone would see it and identify its origin.

Every person who passed the window stopped and gazed at this beautiful glass jug and wondered where it came from and how it got there.

Campbell Barker, a longtime resident of Alpine and one who has spent much time on the Rio Grande, said that he had seen many bottles used by smugglers to take liquor out of Mexico, but that he had never seen such a jug as this one.

Creed Taylor, ex-Texas Ranger and retired Customs Service man said jokingly, "Why don't you know? Roy Stillwell and I hid that jug full of sotol there seventy-five years ago and took turns drinking it up."

Peter Koch, world traveler and lecturer, who makes his home at Big Bend National Park had this to say: "This is a rare bottle. I would say it was made in Spain—perhaps a container for rare wine. I am sure it is valuable as a collector's item."

Dr. Clifford Casey, professor of history at Sul Ross College, said: "That bottle was probably taken away from some priest or monk by the Indians and buried there in the sand. I couldn't say for how long it was buried, but it definitely shows to have been there for many years."

Father Paul Hernandez, a priest who lives at Fort Davis, upon seeing the bottle had this to say: "This is what we call a 'demajuana' in the old country. This type of demajuana was made in Spain as a container for sacramental wine."

He also said that his family in Spain has a demajuana similar to this one, and it is known to be over three hundred years old. He is confident that the two are made from a similar mold.

"These jugs," said Father Hernandez, "were made by hand in small shops in southern Spain where a certain kind of silica is found that is the best material for glass making. The Spaniards learned the art of glass making from the Egyptians. The jugs were made in three pieces, from molds built in the earth. When the molds were made, a test bottle was run off and the measure of the contents taken. Then, in the walls of the mold the metric measurement was imprinted. Each mold was an individual as no two molds could be made identical nor of the same capacity." (This particular demajuana has the numbers "19" followed by smaller size numbers "87" molded near the neck.) "This type of demajuana was made as far back as three thousand years ago and none have been made in the past hundred years. Even in Spain today these demajuanas are rare and considered collectors' items."

Just when this rare demajuana was hidden or buried in the sand dune is speculation. A summing up of evidence would suggest that it has been there for a long time. The reason the bottle had not been found sooner is because a huge cat-claw tree grew over the spot where it was submerged. About four years ago the tree was cut down allowing the sand to shift with the wind, thus uncovering the neck of the bottle.

If you have ever tried to get in under a cat-claw tree with its stickery limbs clinging to the ground, you would readily see why the bottle was bound to have been placed there before the tree grew. This cat-claw tree, with a trunk measuring approximately fifteen inches in diameter, had limbs extending out twelve and fourteen feet from the trunk. It did not grow there overnight. It took many years for a tree to grow to that size in this semi-desert country.

Dr. Barton W. Warnock, botanist at Sul Ross State College, says that it takes more than one hundred years to grow a cat-claw tree to the size of that one since they are of such a slow growth nature.

Referring back to the historical background, learned historians have written that monks and soldiers, religious and secular, marched side by side into the Big Bend Country. Some came from the south. Others came from the north.

Fray Rodriquez introduced the use of the horse to the American Indians. Later he and his companions died at their hands or from illness.

Antonio de Espejo, a wealthy gentleman from Spain, explored the Big Bend Country on his expeditions to New Mexico as well as into Old Mexico along the Conchos in the Presidio area. He found many Indians of the savage Mescalero Apaches and Southern Comanches who were forerunners in the Big Bend region. They continued to harass the white men for years after they came into the region. De Espejo wrote of the different tribes of Indians that he visited and he said that they had well defined trails that led to and from great saline deposits where they obtained their supply of salt. These trails also led to the buffalo country across the Pecos River. He said that the monks assembled as many of the Indians as they could. They erected crosses in their rancheros for them, and by interpreters taught them the meaning of the crosses and the Holy Catholic Faith.

The Spaniards spent two hundred and seventy years in an effort to conquer and colonize this region. The Mexicans threw off the yoke of the Spaniards and upon the crumbling foundation of the Spanish civilization, they, too, attempted to subdue this country. But it remained for the Americans, a northern people with different ideas and ideals to accomplish that which the Spaniards and the Mexicans failed to do.

In view of this, one can only wonder: Did a monk hide this jug of sacramental wine in the sand dune for safekeeping? Or did Indians rob and possibly kill a monk or priest, bury the jug, and then fail to return?

This wine jug is on display at the Hallie Stillwell Hall of Fame Museum on the Stillwell Ranch.

Chief Falling Water

Rex Ivey, "Chief Falling Water" of Lajitas, calls his braves together for a rain dance on *el otro lado*. Lajitas is a village at the bend of the Rio Grande in the Big Bend country. Lajitas in Spanish means "little flat rocks," referring to the Boquillas flagstone one finds in the area. In 1949 Rex bought the trading post established by H. W. McGuirk, the town's leading citizen from 1902 to 1917. The region was inhabited by Mexican Indians, then by Apaches and then by the Comanches. Pancho Villa dominated the region for awhile. Now Rex dominates it. Some may say Rex is contrary. I am not one of them. Rex is a man who forms a considered opinion and has no difficulty maintaining it.

What does Rex say? That is the question asked when rain and weather are discussed in the Big Bend country. And needless to say, when ranchers and farmers get together, that is the first topic gotten out of the way. Here in the Big Bend we don't consult almanacs or weather maps or professional forecasters. We just ask Rex Ivey.

Whether we ship stock or hold on; whether we buy more or sell what we have; whether we go for a picnic or stay home; whether we hang out the weekly wash. Usually all that depends on what Rex says about the weather. His forecasts are just about 100 percent on the mark.

Now if you think rain dances on *el otro lado* are a myth, I would advise that you go down to Lajitas and take a look-see. However, Rex does not depend entirely on the Indian braves and their dances. He knows all the weather signs from thousand-legs climbing the bushes to goats standing with their tails facing one direction to an all cloudy sky with rain pouring down in the middle.

He can tell you if winter will be cold or dry and warm. Simple, he says, just watch the wild animals, the birds and insects — then take a look at the moon, the stars, and the Milky Way — Rex knows all the signs. The lower Big Bend country from Presidio to Judge Roy Bean's Langtry is different from other parts of Texas. For information on events that happened there in the past and what will happen in the future, you can do no better than to ask Rex Ivey. Be it by years or by hours, he can tell you.

Mama, Of All People

Roy Walker "Son" Stillwell could only look at his disheveled eighty-five-year-old mother, clad in hospital garb, shake his head and say hopelessly, "Mama, of all people — ."

Most days of the eighty-five years I have lived have been spent here in the Big Bend, and July 2, 1982, started out not unlike most other days. The Stillwell Ranch is forty-six miles south of Marathon and twenty-five miles north of the Rio Grande. By noon on any given July morning you could fry an egg on a flat rock and serve it up in time for lunch. But on this particular morning, members of my family and my longtime friend Katherine Armstrong had come to join me in visiting my neighbors over in Big Bend National Park. We would get an early start and find food along the way.

The Big Bend region encompasses approximately 20,000 square miles in the southwestern tip of Texas. Big Bend National Park occupies about 1,250 square miles. Three routes can be used to reach the park. One can take State Highway 385 from Fort Stockton through Marathon, or there is Fort Davis through Alpine on Texas 118; or one can go from Marfa to Presidio on U.S. 67, then take FM 170, the "River Road." A semi-circle touching these points is often referred to as the Big Bend of Texas. The Rio Grande forms this bend and hence the name.

From my ranch we drove the six miles over to highway 385 and entered the park at Persimmon Gap. Our first call was on our friends at the park headquarters at Panther Junction. We were a party of six: Katherine, my daughter Dadie Potter, my great

71

grandson Freddie Patton, age twelve, and Dadie's twin granddaughters Chrystal and Jocelyn, age three. I was driving my comfortable and roomy Cadillac. It was old, dependable, and the air conditioning worked great.

We had a fine time visiting at park headquarters and with a stop at Study Butte, to our surprise, we found the afternoon had escaped us. We'd had a satisfactory outing and now we must head for Alpine as the shadows were growing long. I was watching the gathering clouds as they appeared out of nowhere to cap the craggy, awesome Chisos, Rosillos, and Del Carmen Mountains. Rain was falling somewhere, but no way to know where. I picked up my speed as we crossed this section of the Chihuahuan Desert from which these mountain islands rise.

Many creeks and low places (we call them draws) crisscross the mountain ranges and flat desert floor. These watercourses are naturally formed by the run-off from the mountains. Along the highway the draws are marked by water-gauge posts placed to the right or left at the lowest point in the dip to show the traveler the height of the water up to six or ten feet.

The desert around me was bone dry, but I had already made it through two draws with running water without incident. As I topped the rise and started downward into the third draw, my speed was greater than it should have been. As I hit the bottom of the draw, water splashed up onto my engine. We were drowned out! Before I could get the car started again, a wall of water came rushing upon us.

The impact knocked the car crosswise against the water-gauge pole. We adults knew we were in serious trouble. As I assessed the situation I could see that our front wheels were off the concrete dip. The post was all that was holding the car in its precarious position. At any moment we might be swept down the ravine with the now raging waters.

"Mama, what will we do?" Dadie asked.

"Stay with the car, stay with the car," I replied. "Somebody will come to help us."

I knew our only chance to survive was to stay in the car. As long as it stayed lodged against the post and the post held, we might make it out.

Dadie and Katherine put our purses and the twins on the shelf over the back seat. Dadie opened a window so we could get air and then opened the back door so the water could flow through the car. As the water rose higher and higher, panic gripped the children. Freddie began to scream. The twins saw this as the sensible thing to do and joined in. We all prayed as the waves broke over the top of the car and the water rose rapidly inside the car. We saw the back seat float out the door while huge rocks crashed against us as the tremendous power of the water moved everything in its path.

Our prayers were answered. A truck pulled to a stop on the creek bank. As two men jumped out, Dadie screamed, "Save these children, save these children!"

The men went into action in the raging waist-deep water. They skidded and slipped their way over to the stranded car. While Dadie held on for dear life, they opened the other back door and carried the little girls to safety. They returned for Freddie, then Katherine.

Once more we were blessed. A second car came to a stop and saw the rescue efforts. Without hesitation, Dave Cordier, a serviceman from Goodfellow Air Force Base in San Angelo, jumped out to help the exhausted men.

It was Dadie's turn to be taken out. She resisted saying, "Take my mother, take my mother."

"No," the men replied. "She has the steering wheel to hold onto."

Now I was alone in the flooded car. The men were exhausted, and obviously fast action was imperative for me to survive. While my rescue was taking place, Dadie stood in the edge of the water, wanting to help. The men motioned her back, assuring her that they would get me out. However, one of the men did lose his footing in the rampaging water, and she was able to help pull him to safety.

My faith held, and so did the strength of our rescue team. As they opened my car door, the water pulled off my shoes and washed me partially under the car. The men did not stand on ceremony. The serviceman got a hold of me and throwing me over his shoulder like a sack of potatoes, he carried me to the safety of his car. His wife, Pat, who accompanied him, was a trained nurse.

She wrapped me in a blanket and turned the car's heater on to reduce shock.

As this near disaster was taking place, a third car arrived on the opposite side. It was impossible for them to cross over to help, so they turned around and sped back to Study Butte for medical help. John Alexander, a paramedic, and his wife, a nurse, soon arrived in their fully equipped ambulance truck with four-wheel drive.

They drove through the now-subsiding water and transferred us all to the ambulance for the ride back to Study Butte. Before leaving the disaster scene, Mr. Alexander radioed back to park headquarters to report that the Stillwell party was safe. The rangers, who were preparing to send a rescue crew, were relieved at the good news. The rangers said they would contact Son Stillwell in Alpine to come to Study Butte to pick up the family.

While we waited at the clinic, the children's clothes were dried. As much sand, gravel, and mud as possible were removed from each person. As I sat in the clinic, I thanked God for the two courageous fishermen, Melvin and Audivee Weddle, who rescued us. I thought of how often I had cautioned others, "Watch out for water in the creeks, canyons, and draws in this beautiful country; it can be vicious."

When Son stepped into the clinic two hours later and saw his bedraggled family and friend, all he could say was "Mama, of all people—."

Two days later when I finally got back to the ranch and told my younger son Guy my harrowing tale he only shook his head and said, "Mama, of all people—."

Hallie originally wrote this story in the third person. She had observed that Reader's Digest *bought similar stories written in the third person, and she hoped to sell it to them. Betty rewrote the material in the first person.*

Calamity on Chalk Draw

I was pleased that I had a good place to pasture my herd of cattle in 1950. I kept a Mexican man camped there to look after them. I would go every few days to see that everything was being taken care of. I enjoyed my trips and usually took my little granddaughter Marlene along with me.

In the meantime, knowing that my cattle were settled and doing nicely, my writing pal Virginia Madison insisted I come to New York for a visit. I did this and had a marvelous time. Virginia came home with me and the good times continued to roll.

Virginia and I had gone over to the Prude Ranch for dinner and a visit with Johnny Prude. On our way home I noticed a big rain cloud in the direction of Elephant Mountain where I had pastured my herd. I was happy in thinking that I was surely getting a good rain. Early the next morning Virginia and I went to Marfa to watch the filming of the Edna Ferber movie *Giant*. We stopped at the Paisano Hotel to have a cup of coffee before going out to watch the filming, and had a fine time watching the movie stars. Elizabeth Taylor, Rock Hudson, Chill Wills, and James Dean had all come in for their breakfast.

In the meantime a friend from Alpine, Carl Heinman, came to me and said, "I am sorry about your cattle drowning in that rain storm at Elephant Mountain last night." I said to Carl, "You are kidding." He replied, "It's true, Hallie, and I am so sorry." About that time Guy came in and said, "Yes, Mama, our cattle are drowned." What a blow that was! I was devastated. I tried to be normal, but all during that day and for many more to come there were times when I couldn't keep the tears back. It was a subconscious thing. I wouldn't even be aware that I was thinking about the loss. I seemed not to be able to get myself under control. From a financial standpoint the matter was a disaster, and oh, how I grieved for the suffering of my animals.

The Day the Big Horned Billy Goat was Delivered

Word had come to me that Mary Ellen Kimball was looking for some big horned billy goats to put on a mountain so her hunters could shoot at them. I happened to have such an animal that I was very much wanting to get rid of. My experience with this goat was such that I doubted any hunter would connect with him no matter how good a shot he was. Definitely my money was on the goat. And if by chance some hunter did get him, well, I wouldn't lose much time grieving over that. This goat had been a first-class pain to me.

My renegade goat was living on my ranch forty-six miles south of Marathon. He wasn't our goat. He didn't belong to any of our neighbors. I think you could say that he was very much his own goat, a wild outlaw goat, if you will. The problem we were having with him was that he would come down into our ranch headquarters near the beginning of the Maravillas Canyon and encourage our gentle goats to follow after him. Coyotes would eventually devour these gentle goats, then "Old Billy" would come in and pick up some more companions.

Mary Ellen and I had been friends for years. One day I was having lunch at the Bien Venido restaurant in Alpine at the same time Mary Ellen was lunching there. This was my chance. I told her I had exactly the goat she was looking for. She wanted to know how much I wanted for him. I replied, "What will you give?" She offered $35. "Oh," I said, "I'll need to get $50 for him. He's really quite a goat."

Mary Ellen's sense of possession had been whetted, so she agreed to pay the $50. "It will be range delivery," I told her. She said she would send her boys to pick up the goat.

My son Guy was coming in at the end of the week. I thought that since Mary Ellen had actually paid more for the goat than she had intended to, I would have Guy deliver him to her. Also, I was a little concerned as to whether her boys could actually pick up this elusive goat.

Guy penned the billy goat and managed to load him, throwing in another troublesome billy goat for good measure. Guy said that since Mary Ellen was foolish enough to want one goat, she could just take two.

Guy and I drove into Alpine with the two goats in tow. Once loaded they had immediately become adversaries. Our usually pleasant drive had been made something of a trial by an ongoing tussle between them. We consoled ourselves with the thought that soon they would become Mary Ellen's problem.

We arrived at Mary Ellen's place to find that she was not at home. No one was there. Guy inspected her corrals and told me that none of them would hold those two goats. We would have to put them in our backyard at my house in Alpine. I had a good fence that could keep them there until Mary Ellen's boys could pick them up. Guy and I unloaded the goats and put out water for them. Guy went on to do his errands before returning to the ranch. I went in the house to tidy myself. I thought a little nap in the cool of the house might restore my spirit.

As it happened, my spirit would undergo a great deal more anguish before the restoration I longed for. On the way back to my bedroom, I looked out the window to check on my charges. To my horror, my backyard held one goat and one goat only. The long-horned billy goat was nowhere to be seen.

A glance at my watch confirmed my worst fear that the schoolchildren would soon be on the sidewalks on their way home. I ran to my neighbors' houses knocking on doors to ask if they had seen my wayward goat. No one had. I enlisted everyone I could in the search. I was terribly worried that this cranky goat would frighten or even harm a child. He did nothing but eat and fight and not necessarily in that order. I called the police and asked them for help. I called the radio station and ask them to broadcast that a dangerous billy goat was loose in town and that anyone sighting him should please call me. Mary Ellen's sons Gary and Monte heard of my plight and came to help, even though they were less than enthusiastic about their mother's purchase.

I could do nothing more than sit down to wait. Visions of mangled children and myself being hauled into court for harboring dangerous animals floated through my troubled mind. I began to feel that this goat problem would never end.

Nothing lasts forever, and neither did my escaped goat. Soon I got a call from the golf course. My goat had accosted Dr. Tom Coats and Scott Lewis during their weekly afternoon game. Scott chased him down with his golf cart, roped him, and tied him to a water pipe. Thank God. Where but Alpine, Texas, would golfers carry ropes in their golf carts?!

Gary and Monte Kimball came to pick him up. Back in my yard, they tied him securely to a tree. He got loose again, but I found him before he had time to jump the fence. They returned and retied him. The next morning they came to load him and his companion for the trip to their new home. As soon as he was untied, he made one last mad leap toward freedom. Missing the fence, he fell in the well. I went back in the house. I didn't want to know how the boys got him out of that predicament.

Loaded at last, both goats needed to be de-cockleburred before turning them loose on Kimball Mountain. So Gary and Monte went about doing that with their pocketknives. By this time my goats had gained considerable fame in Alpine. The children on their way to school took interest and were distressed thinking the boys were taking their pocketknives to cut up the goats alive. I assured them that no one was going to dismember the living goats and restrained myself from adding that the suggestion was a tempting one.

The two billy goats are relocated on the top of Kimball Mountain and will remain there at least until some city hunter gets a shot at them.

My friend Mary Ellen returned from her vacation to Albuquerque, and she remains my friend. Actually she is quite pleased with the deal we made. The last time I saw Gary and Monte Kimball, they were still trying to wash the eau de goat from their hands and clothes.

Jim Nichols, Pioneer

Jim Nichols, an early homesteader of the Old West, stuck it out and is still around to tell about it. Many homesteaders gave up their claims or sold out to larger landowners when drouth hit and the bottom dropped out of the economy. But a few like Jim Nichols lived out the required time on their land, secured their deeds, and dedicated their lives to building the West.

Jim was born October 2, 1884, to Mr. and Mrs. B. F. Nichols, a Kendall County ranching family. When young Jim came of age to go to school, the family moved to San Antonio and remained there until Jim graduated from San Antonio Academy in 1903.

In the meantime, Jim's sister Malida Jane had married Thomas Dean, a sheetmetal worker from San Antonio. Seeking a more favorable climate for Dean, who had health problems, they explored the Alpine area and found it to be promising. Malida Jane did not want to sacrifice the close relationship she had enjoyed with her parents, so she persuaded both them and Jim to move to Alpine. They chartered an immigrant car from the T&NO Railroad Company, loaded all their possessions, and arrived in Alpine in 1903.

In 1905 Texas School Lands were put up for homesteading. The Act stipulated that the homesteader pay 1/40th of the principal in cash and live on the four sections allowed for three years while accomplishing required improvements. The land cost was set by the Texas Legislature at $1.00 to $1.50 per acre, with the balance on principal carrying a three percent interest rate. Later the allowance was doubled, raising it to eight sections. Jim Nichols acquired his eight sections approximately twenty-five miles northeast of Alpine in Brewster County.

Jim spent months of intense labor developing watering places, building a house, putting up wire fences and constructing barns, corrals, and other improvements. In reminiscing Jim told me, "I hadn't much more than got my house built and a few tanks scraped out until a drouth hit. Tanks went dry, the well I had drilled went dry, and I found myself gathering up old whiskey barrels to use for hauling water. My nearest source for water was the town of Alpine. I had to spend a full day to make a water haul with a wagon and team. Then on arriving at home, I would find half my water sloshed out."

"The first stock that I put on my ranch was a bunch of steers that I bought from Luther Yarbro who ranched in the Marathon area at a community called Pumpkin Center. My father went with me to pick up the steers. We had a pack outfit. We traveled light. We tied our grub on a packhorse and covered it with our only slicker. So then we ran into a big rain with hail. The grub stayed dry, but my father and I were wet to the skin with water running out of our boot tops."

Jim made extra money by taking jobs with other ranchers during slack times on his own ranch. Joe Irving, who ranched in the Glass Mountains, hired him to help round up 2,500 steers. He recalls that their horns were so large they had to be turned sideways to be loaded in cattle cars.

In 1915 Jim married Martha Elizabeth Johnson, a native of Palo Pinto County, who had come to Alpine with her family only two years before. Jim and Martha had four children, three of whom are still living. Their son Harold is business manager for Victoria College. Another son called Buzz, and a daughter, Mrs. Jesse James, live in Pecos.

Jim lasted out the drouth and depression of the early thirties. With the bettering economy, he built more ranch improvements, including a fine house, more tanks, and good wells that piped water over his ranch land. He was in good shape to weather the drouth of the fifties and came out of it better than many of his neighbors.

Even though the work was hard, Jim enjoyed his many years of ranching. He feels now the time has come for him to take life a bit easier and concentrate on things that are fun. Like keeping up with baseball. So late in summer of this year, Jim sold off all his livestock. Then he sold his land to W. Y. Benge III of Carrizozo, New Mexico, thus ending fifty-four years of homestead ranching in West Texas.

A Local Project

Fools rush in where angels fear to tread is an old saying that I have reason to believe was originated as a warning just for me. A warning, I might add, that I never seem to have enough sense to heed! Such was the case in the early spring of 1955 when I started probing into why a Hispanic boy quit school on the eve of his graduation.

Seeing our star basketball player on the street at ten o'clock on Monday morning, I was very much surprised, for only a couple of nights before I had watched him do more than his part to win a basketball game. I determined to find out why he was not in school.

Johnny Muniz was Hispanic, and I realized that often the Hispanics dropped out of school before graduating. I went to the school and asked the superintendent why Johnny was not in attendance. He explained that the boy was twenty years old and was getting married. "But why," I asked, "is he twenty years old and still in school?" The superintendent replied that, "Hispanics are slow to learn."

This couldn't be the complete answer. I knew all in the family to be of above average intelligence. Even so, I was aware that they had a hard time making a living and that this probably contributed to the fact that Johnny had quit school. Moreover, as is the general rule in such families, there were a number of younger children also to be fed, clothed, and educated.

Next I talked to a woman who had taught school in Marathon for the past forty years. From her I learned another reason why a twenty-year-old would still be in high school. Hispanic children do not start to school in the first grade as Anglo children do. They are started in the pre-primer. This information brought my next question. Why start Hispanic children in the pre-primer and Anglo children in the first grade when all the children are the same age when they start school? The answer given was the Hispanic children speak little or no English, and the pre-primer is a class to acquaint them with the English language. By the end of the year, I found to my horror, only fifty percent of them would be ready to start first grade.

Wondering aloud why this situation had been allowed to exist, I was dismayed to hear the teacher say that several years ago, when effort had been made to improve the standard of education for Hispanics, a local landowner had said it would only ruin a lot of good sheepherders! In other words, the best way to keep cheap labor was to keep uneducated labor. I felt ashamed of being an Anglo!

I began to search my mind for a solution. If the little children have to go to language school, so to speak, why not send them when they are five, and by doing so, give them a "leg-up" to start first grade on a more equal footing with the Anglo children. I had heard of summer residents who did a great deal for local Mexican families while living in our community. If they were interested in their welfare in summer maybe they would be in winter, too. One man had supposedly put a Mexican boy through college. I made an appointment to talk with him. He was gracious and thought the kindergarten a most worthy project. But just as graciously, he declined to give a cent. It seems he felt that the boy he had helped through college had not been sufficiently grateful. (In the meantime I have learned that the boy repaid his debt in full.) I was really disappointed, for I had been sure this man would give at least $1,000 for the school.

Many of the people who have lived in our area all their lives could underwrite a kindergarten, but I knew it was useless to ask for financial help from any of them. Still another summer resident, a woman of independent means, had not been approached. I made an appointment with this woman, and although considerably intimidated, I kept it. Words stuck in my mouth. My previous interview and the man's "no" kept flitting through my mind. But the woman had already heard about my project from a mutual Hispanic friend.

Her first words struck terror in my heart. "My dear," she said, "tell me about your organization." I thought that over. Finally I confessed that we had no money, no organization, nothing but an idea. She told me that money is secondary. She said I should go home and get organized and then return. I was disappointed, but I knew she was right.

I went home and had barely closed the door when the phone rang. It was the woman I had just left, and again she opened the conversation with "My dear." This time, however, her next words were music to my ears. She said, "I realize you do need money to get started, and I am putting a check for two months' salary in the mail right now. You can count on me for more if you need it."

My mind quickly did the math. Two months down and seven months to go! Who would give the other seven? Well, Roy and I could give one of them! This woman's gift had given me confidence. I found others who were interested in helping. We "organized," and I found myself chairman of the board.

The local VFW, which consists of a majority of Hispanic veterans, had pledged their support. Now they started to work in earnest. They told us we could have their building for a classroom. They even put in a partition that provided a large room for classes and a smaller room for showing films. These veterans worked like beavers. At night and on Saturdays they would gather and work on the building. At last it was ready for paint and floor covering.

Our next move was to find a teacher. This came easily. A young Hispanic girl, born and reared with Spanish-speaking people, applied for the job. She had taught pre-primer at a small school for Hispanics on the Rio Grande for three years. She lacked only a few hours having her college degree. She agreed to teach for $150 a month because she would have a chance to complete her degree at a nearby teacher's college while living at home. We checked her references and found she was considered to be an excellent teacher and one the local Hispanic population had confidence in. Many of our local Hispanic people are timid with us, and we felt fortunate to have a teacher whom they knew and loved.

The Roman Catholic priest, knowing the insecurity of the people, was very much interested in getting the school started. When he heard we needed financial assistance, he donated $25 and spent much time and effort contacting parents to persuade them to take advantage of the benefits the school would offer.

Unexpected problems arose daily. The first requirement was to obtain water for the building. We asked several people who lived nearby about using their water, but we got no cooperation. Almost at the point of giving up, we learned that the building had always obtained water from the man who owned the property across the street. After considerable effort, we located him. He said that his well had never been strong, but we were welcome to use it until it ran dry. We assured him we would use only enough for drinking, washing hands, and flushing the toilets.

We made the decision to paint the old floor rather than put down new. Two old kitchen tables were donated. The legs were cut off to make them child-size. The county judge had a small sum of money to be spent within the county. He told us to make a list of supplies we would need up to $100, and he would order them as well as twelve child-sized chairs. More chairs were needed, so I called the chairman of the deacons at the Baptist church and acquired eight additional chairs there.

We were ready for opening day. The community was curious, and we expected a crowd. We were not disappointed, for nearly everyone in town came. Much to their surprise, they found us as well equipped as the public schools. People who had been skeptical in the beginning were now encouraging and enthusiastic.

Our school opened the same day public school opened. We considered our kindergarten "public," for we hoped to operate entirely without tuition. Every eligible Hispanic child in Marathon enrolled except for one. Not only did the Hispanic five-year-olds enroll; we had two Anglo children enroll. This was a pleasant surprise. Our lower grades in the public school were segregated, so we felt mixing the English-speaking children with the Spanish-speaking children would help the language problem.

Christmas came, and our school put on a program. The children sang songs in English, made short speeches, and presented a Christmas play. Santa rewarded them with gifts of dolls, toy cars, candy, and fruit. We all wore pleased expressions on our faces.

At the close of the school term in May, the kindergarten held commencement exercises. Each child wore a cap and gown and received his or her diploma. The house was full and everyone was proud of our kindergarten. And none more than I!

As I left the school building, my thoughts were of the future. Would the school be able to continue as it had this first year? We made effort to have our school affiliated with the public school without success. Texas had passed a law in 1949 that a local school board has to maintain a kindergarten in a community if as many as twenty-five parents sign a petition and present it to the school board between June 1 and August 31. We didn't have twenty-five parents who had five-year-olds.

Now it is mid-term in our second year. Our teacher's salary is paid until March first. We have a balance of six dollars in the bank. Last night the phone rang. Our treasurer was calling to say we would have to call a special meeting and vote to close the kindergarten. We met. In a few minutes we had raised still another month's salary. Somehow we will continue to meet this special need in our community.

The Ghost Lights of the Big Bend

If seeing is believing, unless you have seen the ghost lights in the mountains of the Big Bend country, you will find it hard to believe these lights really do exist and shine brightly at certain times.

I first saw the ghost lights in the Chinati Mountains southwest of Marfa in the Shafter area and in the Cienegas during 1916 and 1917. I was teaching school in Presidio at the time and made many trips back and forth from Presidio to Alpine. Mostly I traveled at night because by the time school was dismissed and I would get up the road, it would be dark. Back in those days roads were not paved, and it would take half a day to go from Presidio to Marfa, a distance of only sixty miles.

I have seen ghost lights in the "Dead Horse Mountains" (Caballos Muertos) in the southern part of Brewster County and in the Santiago Range between Dog Canyon and the Rio Grande.

I have talked to many people who have seen these lights. Mrs. Otis Lee of Alpine said that while she and her husband were living in the area of the Dead Horse Mountains, they saw the lights many times.

W. G. Fielder of Alpine, one of the old timers in the Big Bend, has seen the mysterious lights on many occasions and says of them, "I cannot tell why, how, or what, but the lights are there."

To many the lights are frightening. When my sister Glen Harris saw the light on the Dead Horse Mountains she was so frightened that she wouldn't get out of the car to open the gate. This happened one dark night as we were returning to the Stillwell Ranch from Marathon. The dull red light appeared suddenly, flickering along the sides of the mountain, sometimes flaring up brightly, then disappearing only to come back again in another place. Many ranch people have seen this light. The Albert Chambers family lived in the vicinity of the Dead Horse for many years. They say they often saw the light as they sat in their yard at night before bedtime. It always appeared in the same direction on the same side of the mountain.

Just recently my son Guy Stillwell and his wife Diane were returning to Stillwell Ranch from Marathon. Suddenly the light appeared so bright and so near that they feared they would be hit by a ball of fire. But, upon regaining their composure, they determined that the light was like the one seen so many times on the Dead Horse Mountains, except that it seemed to be farther to the east than usual.

The lights seen when traveling between Marfa and Alpine on Highway 90 looking south appear to be near the Cienega Mountains. I have seen these lights several times. They are seen more often than the others because more people travel Highway 90.

Bernal Slight, pioneer resident of Alpine, says he has seen the lights often. He offers no explanation. "They're just there," he says.

Mrs. Jim Casner, another long-time resident, says she has seen the ghost light many times south of the highway between Marfa and Alpine in the vicinity of the Cienegas. "It is just a weird light that flickers, sometime flaring up brightly, then dimming. At times it looks like the headlight of a train," says Mrs. Casner.

Mrs. W. D. Burcham of Alpine taught school in Shafter in 1915 and 1916. She said that she saw the ghost lights in the Chinatis many times while traveling at night between her job in Shafter and her home in Alpine. Mrs. Burcham is of the opinion that the lights are caused by rocks that are fluorescent and shine when cosmic rays make contact.

W. D. Smithers, noted writer, photographer, and historian of the Big Bend country, says that the lights are due to natural causes. "No one knows exactly how they are caused, but facts gathered from such men as surveyors, rangers, and other out-of-doors men, indicate that they are freaks of nature caused by climatic conditions and mineral elements. Most of them have been traced to mountains where there are caves that contain guano that produces a flame-like glow at night."

During border trouble days, when Smithers traveled over the Big Bend with pack trains and wagon trains, he would see a glow coming out of the canyons which would last probably an hour. He and the men with the trains presumed the lights to be chemical action from minerals in the rocks in the canyons.

The mysterious lights or ghost lights or whatever one would call them come and go at times as mysteriously as their existence. Some day the mystery may be solved, but up to this time those who have seen with their own eyes accept the fact that the lights exist and leave the explanation to the future.

Hallie on Cows

Cows are just like people. They really are. Take a general roundup of cattle on the ranch, and you'll have the equal to a farmers' convention or a meeting of the Ladies' Aid Society.

Being an old cowpuncher, I've often entertained myself while holding the herd by comparing cows with people. Just the other day I was watching an old cow in the herd. She was real puny and shy. She kept sidling off away from the herd. I reckoned she had just come through a difficult time raising a foxy heifer calf with little grass to keep her fat. She really didn't want to mix with the herd and be looked at and talked about. She acted like she was half ashamed of herself just like a woman will act when you catch her without her hair combed and her lipstick on.

On the other hand, there was a fat young mother cow that came strutting into the middle of the herd with her fine bull calf following. She was as friendly and happy as a woman with a brand new hat.

Some old cows are naturally meek and timid. Either they hang behind or try to sneak out of the herd. Others are natural-born leaders. They can help you out by leading the rest right into the corral. Or they can lead them off into a thicket where you don't want them to go. The good leader cow is an asset if you hold a tight check on her. Just the same as some people are leaders and will do a lot of good if they hold to the right course.

Cows pick their own companions and choose the place to hang out on the range just as people choose their friends and places to live. Cows have habits, and they exercise them as regularly as clockwork. Some roam to the far end of the pasture and stay out as long as they can. Others stay close to water. You can bet your life they'll be right there day after day. So do some people travel to the far corners of the world while others stay right at home year in and year out.

A few days ago two of my milch cows had calves. One little feller is just as gentle as a lamb. The first time I put him in the pen he would suck my finger and let me pet him. The other calf was born wild-eyed and skittish. She won't allow anyone to pet her, and she manages to get out of the pen everyday. Calves, like babies, will make friends with anybody or bawl and squall when a stranger looks at them.

Some old cows are so wild and mean to handle we have to sell them before they ruin the good habits and disposition of the other cows. Just like we have to get rid of people that go wild. Butcher shops for onery cows and jails for onery people.

Yes, I think that cows and people are a lot alike.

The Big Horse Race in Ojinaga

Among spectators at a horse race there is always a lot of tension, but where men will bet the boots off their feet, the saddles off their horses, and their ranches right out from under their families on a race between two horses, the spectators are unanimously afflicted with hypertension. And those still around to tell about the big horse race in Ojinaga, Mexico, back in 1892 haven't gotten over it yet.

It was a matched race between a horse from Mexico and a horse from Texas at 400 yards for a $10,000 purse. The owners of the horses put up $5,000 apiece. In those days no individual on the frontier had that kind of money; so friends staked all they had on the horse they believed would win by helping the owner make up his share of the purse. There were plenty of side bets, too, with the stakes running the gamut from boots to brides and from ranches to silver mines.

The whole thing started when Dan Knight, the sheriff of Presidio County, Texas, went to Chihuahua, Mexico for a Cinco de

Mayo celebration and saw a good looking quarter horse belonging to one Don Rafael winning every race he ran and making more money than a sheriff would make in a lifetime.

The sheriff knew a horse breeder in San Antonio who raised some fine race horses and he figured that if he could buy one, it would do to match with Don Rafael's money maker. For $400 he made the deal. That wasn't much for a good race horse, even in those days. The only trouble was that this particular horse was cold jawed, wild, and hard to start. But Sheriff Knight had seen him run and getting him started was the gamble he had to take.

He kept his plans under his hat. He shipped the horse to Marfa and rode him to Presidio, Texas, which is situated on the Rio Grande just across the river from Ojinaga, Mexico. There he turned the horse over to a couple of his friends, the Spencer brothers, to keep on their farm and began looking around for a man to train his prospective race horse. At a ranch round-up, he saw a 14-year-old kid, Jim Walker, ride up looking for a job. When he saw how the boy handled horses, he hired him and without tipping his hand to anybody took Jim down to Presidio to train his horse.

From that day until the day of the big race, Jim was virtually a prisoner. He had to eat, drink, and sleep with that horse and he was not allowed to talk to anyone about his bedfellow. Even Jim didn't know where the horse came from. All he had to do was to teach him to start at a given point and run a certain distance in the shortest possible time. Jim said, "The first time I got on that fool horse, I thought he was *loco*. He didn't like starting lines and when he got started I couldn't stop him. But somehow he took a liking to me and in two months he calmed down and I could handle him like a Mexican handles a tortilla."

When the sheriff saw how his horse was working out he began to put out talk that his horse could beat anything on the border. The rumor spread on both sides of the Rio Grande and it wasn't long before Don Rafael took the bait and offered to match a race with the sheriff's horse. The two got together on the deal and set a time and place for the race.

Mexicans from Ojinaga slipped over the Rio Grande to get a look at the horse that the Texans were saying could beat Don Rafael's horse, which by now was the pride of all Chihuahua. But nobody got a glimpse of the Texas horse in action and what they saw dozing in the sun was enough to make them bet their boots off on the horse from Ojinaga.

Jim worked out the little quarter horse but no one saw him. Those who got a look at the rough looking nag didn't say anything about him for they didn't want to damage their chances to make a good bet, but secretly they were laughing up their sleeves at the Texans who thought they had a good horse.

As the time for the race drew near, the excitement mounted. Rumors spread, attributing the most fantastic fleetness to the favorite of the individuals putting out the rumor. So effective was this advertising that before the day for the big race rolled around every man in the Big Bend country, and almost the entire population of both sexes for miles around Ojinaga, were set to be spectators.

The Mexican women embroidered a silk robe to be given to the winner. The track was made hard and fast, watered down by hand with water carried in *ollas* from the Rio Grande and smoothed with sage brush branches. The track was watered and swept every day for a week. The Mexican army was alerted to handle the crowds which began gathering days before the race. Plenty of tequila and sotol was lugged in by burro back in goat skins, and the men primed themselves well and often until plans for the celebration after the race equaled any Cinco de Mayo fiesta ever held in Ojinaga.

As the hour of one o'clock approached on the day of the race the crowds were in a festive mood. Bets were made loud and public. *Mucho dinero* was going on the nose of El Caballo de Don Rafael. One young Mexican arrived in a fancy buckboard teamed by two good horses and riding with him was his bride to be. He bet the whole rig against enough money to set the young couple up for housekeeping. If he lost, the bride would have to wait a year or more for her wedding day. A lot of futures were riding on that big race. One old prospector staked his claim in the silver mine country at Shafter against a patch of corn near Ojinaga. And many a cowboy from the Texas side bet his month's wages against those of the cowboys of Mexico. There are no records of how much money changed hands that day, but the horse from Mexico was the favorite by a long shot.

The owners of the two horses literally laid their money on the line. The $10,000 purse was hauled onto the track at the starting line and dumped on the ground. Every denomination under the sun made up that pile of money. Mexican pesos and American dollars — paper money, gold, and even silver and copper — indicated that a lot of barrel bottoms had been scraped to fill the obligations and honor the bets. Those who bet just for the fun of it at big race tracks and watch their favorites spring simultaneously with a whole field of horses from starting gates electrically operated can't possibly understand the excitement and tension that charges the air where men bet everything they own on a matched horse race.

The money was ready and the crowd was ready. When the horses were brought onto the track the crowd surged forward, most of them getting their first glimpse of the sheriff's horse. What they saw made a lot of bettors wish they had kept their mouths shut and caused others to attempt to recoup what was sure to be a loss by making ridiculous last minute bets.

The horses approached the track from different directions and when they caught sight of each other for the first time, the action started. The sheriff's horse laid back his ears, which made him look exactly like a mule. The Mexican horse stopped dead in his tracks, his front feet planted wide apart and his nostrils flared. His beautiful sleek sides quivered and he ran backwards a few yards before he turned tail and bolted. A gasp went up from the crowd when the horse handlers had to get horses to go after the favorite and literally drag him back to the track. The Texas horse was reined calmly toward the starting line. Some who saw that meeting of the two horses thought the Mexican horse was frightened by the noisy crowd pushing onto the track, but those who understand horses knew that the Mexican horse was just scared of the other horse.

With the unexpected stampede of the favorite, the crowd went wild. The Mexican army couldn't control them, and the owners of the horses had to postpone the race until they could fence the track with lechuguilla rope. The delay created more tension and the spectators began to speculate on the ability of the jockeys. Jim Walker, who had trained the sheriff's horse, was to ride him in the race. Both jockeys were about the same age — fourteen — and they were mounted barefooted, strapped to the horse with a sursingle, which made it impossible for them to do anything but ride. The Mexican jockey weighed 84 pounds and Jim weighed 64 pounds. No one suggested a weight handicap because, to most of those present, it looked as if the Texas horse had been foaled with all the handicap he could carry.

The jockeys tossed a coin to decide which one would do the asking for the start. The jockey from Ojinaga won the toss. They made several starts but the Mexican jockey failed to ask "Ready?" Jim could see that his horse was starting better than the famous race horse from Ojinaga. Finally, the Mexican jockey yelled, "Ready?" and Jim answered, "Ready." The Texas horse took the bit in his mouth and bolted. Before Jim could get his breath, the race was over. The crowd cheered and surged forward pushing money into Jim's hands and his pockets. His cap was pulled off and stuffed with money, too. Suddenly Jim Walker was a hero — his independence won with the horse race. The silken robe was laid on the back of the sheriff's horse and the victory march was started. The Texans tried to stop the parade for they were expecting trouble. The lives of the people of Ojinaga and surrounding territories had been filled for weeks with nothing but the big race and now they and their idol had lost and the Texas horse was wearing the trophy which no one had expected to cross the Rio Grande as a prize.

But Jim Walker said the Mexicans were the best losers he ever saw. There was no grumbling about the way the race was run nor did they question the outcome. If they were disappointed they didn't show it and some of them had lost all they had. The Mexican army guarded the jockey from Texas as he rode his fleet footed mount directly behind the band which led the parade for hours. At intervals women pushed forward to give Jim flowers — some were made of paper. Everywhere the admiring Mexicans called out the name of the new victor — La Golandrina (the swallow or swift) — and the little 64-pound jockey sat proudly on his mount enjoying what he called the "happiest day of my life."

Later Jim was paid $5 to have his picture made wearing his Sunday clothes with a colorful handkerchief around is neck and big bright stockings pulled neat and tight over his knees. His best shoes, with worn soles flapping loose, were shined for the occasion. He posed with his hand on his hip and the Mexican jockey on his horse next him. That picture of the victor and the vanquished is a masterpiece of photography.

After the race, La Golandrina was given to the Spencer brothers at Presidio. The sheriff had a sizeable nest egg, and Jim

Walker's reputation as a horse handler was made Everybody joined wholeheartedly in a real border celebration. To this day, when Big Benders start talking about horse races you can bet your bottom dollar that some one will come up with, "Did you ever hear about the big horse race down in Ojinaga in 1892?"

HALLIE THE JUDGE

On March 20, 1964, the *Odessa American* ran a story on Hallie Stillwell's appointment as Justice of the Peace for Brewster County under the banner headline "Alpine Woman Named." Hallie told me the story this way:

"I was still living with the Bensons in Alpine and driving Gene part of the time, and I had taken a full-time job managing the coffee shop at the Holland Hotel. The county commissioners took their morning coffee break there and one morning the conversation centered on the shocking news that Justice of the Peace Jim Parker had died suddenly from a heart attack. Distress over the loss of a friend and sympathy for the family were expressed by all of us. I had gone on about my work as the commissioners began to talk about the necessity of an immediate replacement for the position. Distances were too great for a neighboring JP to assume the duties even for a few days. Someone must be found to take responsibility right away. By this time I had seated myself at the cash register. One of the commissioners looked my way and remarked that Hallie could do it. 'Do what?' I asked. And before I really had time to consider, they had me convinced that I could be a justice of the peace.

"I accepted the appointment for Mr. Parker's unexpired term, and then I ran on my own in the May 2 Democratic primary and was elected. No one ran against me in the general election. So that next January I became Alpine's first elected woman justice of the peace. And I kept the position for fourteen years. I always tried to render justice fairly and impartially. The weddings were the part I enjoyed most. And there were sad things I had to do, like informing grief-stricken parents of the deaths of their children. And trying to settle disputes between good people was not always easy. One time Inda Benson, my best friend, got a speeding ticket. Well, nobody knew better than I did that Inda drove over the speed limit, and I had to fine her the maximum. On one occasion Alpine's mayor had celebrated a little too enthusiastically. He got a DWI, and I had to fine him $200. And there were the grandchildren and the nieces and nephews. Seems like I always had some of the family up before me. It got to the point that every Monday morning I would go in and find a stack of tickets on my desk. These were tickets written over the weekend. The weekends were when the younger folks liked to party. Well, the first thing I did was to go through the stack and set aside all the tickets that belonged to any member of my family. I didn't know about the circumstances of the other folks, but I knew that the members of my family had been taught to behave properly. They knew better than to go around breaking the law. So right then I assigned the maximum penalty to them. I considered all the other cases on an individual basis because I didn't know if those people had had the advantage of being taught to behave properly. So I would talk to them and make my decision on the basis of their responses."

Hallie did not exempt herself from the law either. Once an Alpine resident pointed out that he had seen her run a red light. She was unaware that she had done so, but she took his word for it and fined herself.

"When my grandson Frank got old enough to go to high school, I was living in Dadie's Alpine house," she continued. "Frank came in to live with me through the week so he wouldn't have to drive to school from the ranch every day. He was a good kid, but he was energetic, and all that energy got him into trouble just like it does all kids. He had already paid off a long string of maximum fines when he and a pal got into trouble again for driving too fast and disturbing the peace. So this time when I fined them the maximum, they said they couldn't see their way clear to pay the fine, and they'd just lay it out in jail. I told them that the matter was entirely up to them. I offered to go their bail if they wanted me to. But they said no; they'd go to jail. So the sheriff took them over and locked them up. The weather was hot, and the jail's air conditioning wasn't working very well. And there was no television, nothing to do but play dominoes or look at an old magazine. They stuck it out for the better part of the day. But before time for me to take off work, they were calling for me to come get them out. I did. The whole episode turned out to be a lot harder on me than on them. I had suspended Frank's driver's license. So then I had to drive him everywhere he had to go."

Hallie always said that performing wedding ceremonies was the part she enjoyed most, and she carried that function on into retirement. She fondly recalled one very young couple who came before her to be married. She counseled them on the gravity of assuming marital responsibilities and their natural consequences — not your run-of-the-mill justice of the peace chore — but she threw it in at no extra charge. After ascertaining to her satisfaction that they had seriously considered their impending action, she performed the ceremony. On concluding, she told the young man, "Now you may kiss your bride." He smiled at her slyly and said, "I did already."

In 1999 former Brewster County Attorney Richard E. Bowers, who shared courthouse office space with Hallie during her years as JP, recalled the following.

"Because our district covered such an unmanageable amount of territory, Hallie was often called upon to do chores that did not rightfully belong to her job," Bowers told me. "The hardship of the office was that she was called out at any time of the day or night to go to a remote area and pronounce someone dead. In these cases she was absolutely fearless. And she could go anywhere she was called without getting lost. She knew every inch of Brewster County," he said.

Mr. Bowers also said that the aspect of the job that she dreaded most was the day she had to make her books balance; that is, the amount of cash she had deposited had to match the receipts she had written.

"Paperwork was not Hallie's forte," he said. "She loved to talk to people, and her habit was to open the drawer wherever she happened to be standing and stuff the money into it while she was carrying on her conversation. Consequently on the day of reckoning, she had to go through all the drawers looking for money. Any shortfall had to be made up from her own pocket. And there were always a certain number who were paying on her homemade installment plan."

While Hallie trusted many people to pay their fines as promised, only one person ever let her down, which she figured was a pretty good record. She said that once a man from Houston was picked up for speeding on Christmas Eve. He could not pay his fine, but faithfully promised Hallie that his mother would send the money as soon as he reached Houston. The mother did send the money and a note to Hallie thanking her for trusting her son and saying how much having him with the family on Christmas Day had meant to her.

Hallie stayed on the job as justice of the peace from 1964 until 1978. She enjoyed the years she served as justice of the peace, and the income the job provided was a godsend in the struggle to recover from the drouthy fifties. By 1978 family finances were easier. She felt that she was ready to retire and return to the ranch. On her retirement, the Alpine community gave her a wonderful retirement party and, as a "thank you" gift for her many years of service, they presented her with a check for $1,000 to be applied to an airline ticket to "anywhere in the world you want to go." Hallie chose England. Dadie was teaching in San Antonio at the time, so she took Hallie to the airport and put her on a plane. English acquaintances whom Hallie had befriended while they were visiting the ranch met her at the airport in London. These friends were thrilled to have the opportunity to return the Stillwell hospitality. They did their best to see that Hallie didn't miss a thing. She even got to see the estate where the opera singer Lily Pons lived. Miss Pons, remarkably, had visited the Stillwell Ranch in 1956. An admirer had told the famous diva that the truth was that she, not Lily Langtry, had been the fantasy love of Judge Roy Bean. So en route from San Antonio to San Angelo, she stopped to visit Langtry and the Jersey Lily. Somehow she and Hallie happened onto the same event. A clipping from the May 3, 1956, *El Paso Times* shows both stars finely dressed and radiating glamour. The story notes that Miss Pons had accepted Hallie's invitation to visit her ranch. Had she not been off on a concert tour, Miss Pons no doubt would have been delighted to receive Hallie in England.

Hallie wrote at least nine three-by-five index cards of her recollections as justice of the peace. Unfortunately, all have been lost except for cards numbered eight and nine, cited here:

> ...of weeks he and his girl came into my office with license in hand and I married them. They are still very happy.

96

I have performed two weddings at Fort Davis State Park at the top of the scenic drive; two weddings at Stillwell Trailer Park, one at Big Bend National Park, one at the Chili Cook-off at Terlingua, two at Terlingua Ranch, and two in San Antonio.

I performed the ceremony for a couple who were college students. They had just graduated. After two years they came into my office and requested another marriage ceremony. I was at a loss for words and asked what the trouble was. They said there was no trouble. They were so happy they wanted to go through it all again. So they had blood tests, got a license, and had the same ceremony. I have not seen them since.

One of the last wedding ceremonies that I performed was an El Paso couple who wanted to be married at Santa Elena Canyon, more than 100 miles south of Alpine. Would I go there? Yes, and I drove by myself to the canyon. They said they loved that area. They had been there many times, and they wanted to be married there. As I left them after the ceremony I looked back to see them arm in arm gazing at the high canyon walls above the waters of the Rio Grande...

The marriages Hallie performed at the Terlingua Festival are well documented from several different sources. Caliente Chili Company of Austin issued the following press release, which is not cited in its entirety:

On November 1, 1975, at high noon in the Terlingua Chapel, Terlingua, Texas, during the 9th Annual Wick Fowler Memorial Chili Cookoff, the marriage of Nancy and Pete will be consummated. The official chili queen, Judge Hallie Stillwell, from Alpine, Texas, will perform the wedding vows.

Although mock weddings (to last only for the duration of a chili event) have been performed at cookoffs, this will be the first authentic wedding at the world's cookoff. Hopefully the marriage will last longer than the two-day event of this, the only bonafide world championship chili cookoff.

The bride, given in marriage by all the Fowlers, will wear the traditional red and white ground-length wedding gown and carry a bouquet of chili peppers arranged with red velvet ribbons. Mother of the bride will wear a formal red and white mother's dress. The attire for the groom and bride's father will be red satin coats with tails, chili pepper boutonnieres, and red western hats. The sons of the bride and groom will wear tuxedo T-shirts and red Texas Hatter's specials. Jackie Gannaway of Austin designed the original wedding ensemble.

Sometime following the wedding, there will be a reception at the Terlingua Hondo Hilton. Free samples of chili will be provided by contestants of the cookoff.

Music for both the wedding and reception will be attempted by a 150-piece orchestra, "The Study Butte Metropolitan Music Massacre and Chorus," under arrangement and direction of Robert "Yellow Dog" Marsh of San Antonio.

After the guests express their good luck wishes by throwing chili peppers and pinto beans at the newlyweds, the bride and groom (including all relatives) will have a brief wedding trip to Mexico (Boquillas). Travel arrangements via burro have been scheduled by Fritz of Fest Travel Agency of Fredericksburg and are contingent upon the Rio Grande not being on the rise.

The newlyweds will reside somewhere in Austin providing they survive the wedding. Of course, all wedding plans are depending on Nancy obtaining approval of her request for five days sick leave from her employer — and Pete showing up.

Nancy Fowler Sebastian is the niece of Wick Fowler.

Hallie performed another marriage at the Chili Festival in 1984. The *San Angelo Standard-Times* reported the event in its November 9 edition as follows, in a story by Bud McDonald:

In the midst of madness during the annual autumn rite of chili cookery in the remote desert ghost town, a Washington couple was joined in holy matrimony.

A whooping and hollering crowd of about 1,000 somewhat less than sober chiliheads became quietly solemn as 88-year-old Hallie Stillwell, retired Brewster County justice of the peace, spoke the familiar binding words over Dr. Doug Wilkey and Cathy Bruce, both of Seattle, Washington.

Wilkey, a dental surgeon and head cook of the Dogbreath Chili Team, said the Terlingua International Chili Cookoff seemed an appropriate wedding site.

"We met in 1982 while both of us were entered in a chili cookoff at Mukilteo, Washington," said Wilkey. "I liked her right off, even though we were on competing teams."

Mrs. Wilkey joined the Dogbreath Chili Team that year. Apparently the union was a good one, as the team won the Oregon State Chili Cookoff that year and a similar cookoff in Canada in 1983....

The wedding was a popular break for the crowd, but Ms. Stillwell was the obvious star of the show. Although she retired from the Brewster County bench in 1978 at the age of 82, Ms. Stillwell is not fazed by chili tournaments and other events of tomfoolery.

"I judged the first cookoff in 1967 between Wick Fowler and H. Allen Smith who started all this foolishness," Ms. Stillwell said.

Although Ms. Stillwell is no longer a justice of the peace, her powers to conduct marriage ceremonies remain through her life.

"Everything's legal and above board," she said.

HALLIE AND THE STILLWELL RV PARK

Legend has it that Roy Stillwell, a renowned shot, announced in the preplanning days of Big Bend National Park that he would shoot the first government S.O.B. that set foot on Stillwell Ranch. Perhaps for that reason the eastern perimeter of Big Bend National Park borders on the western perimeter of the Stillwell Ranch. Hallie had long dreamed of establishing a convenience store and RV park on a small strip of land separated by Highway 2627 from the rest of the ranch. This is a sightly piece of land, which meanders from a high hill overlooking the spread down to Black Gap Wildlife Refuge. On the western side, hills abut the park, and on the eastern side, a dirt road leads some six or seven miles down to the old ranch headquarters and Maravillas Canyon. Stillwell Mountain is in the background. The suitability of this land for that purpose was obvious, but Hallie had never managed to accumulate the funds necessary to realize her dream.

Hallie's brother Alvin had long lived in California. He and his family had "done well." They sympathized with Hallie in her struggle to hold on to the ranch, and they remembered her long years of indebtedness to the bank and her great fear of losing her land. They understood her reluctance to go into debt again.

Shortly after a visit from Alvin's son Bob, in 1967, Hallie received a letter with a check enclosed in the amount of $5,000. Bob wrote that the money was not a loan, and no strings were attached to it. Its only purpose was to help establish the RV park. God bless Bob! She did exactly that. She built an adobe structure for the convenience store that included a living area in back. It had a front porch for folks to sit on. Hookups were built nearby that provided electricity and fresh well water to campers. "Public showers and rustic camping" were offered, too. Rustic camping meant you could take your bedroll out and pick a spot somewhere on 22,000 acres, unroll it and lie down. The showers went like hotcakes!

In the early years Hallie kept her job as JP in Alpine. To manage her RV park and convenience store, she went to Marathon and found another cowboy charmer in the person of Son Lee. Son went down to the ranch and began to build the business and unlikely social center that is now Stillwell Store and RV Park. If not actually bilingual, Son was an affable fellow who easily made himself understood in cowboy English and Tex-Mex Spanish. In no time at all, he had built a decent border trade in goods and gasoline. Big Bend neighbors came from miles around for gas, bread, eggs, and ice, as their needs required. They stayed on to exchange news. The sight of a next-door neighbor landing his plane on Highway 2627 to pick up a case of beer and a bag of chips was a common event. After a good visit he would take off as he landed, down the road. Dominoes appeared on the porch tables and games of 42 and 88 were common entertainment. Campers extended their visits a day or two to savor the West Texas atmosphere. This open and friendly attitude infused the Stillwell Stores' environment from opening day, and it remains there to this day.

In time Hallie's youngest sister, Glen, moved a mobile home to the ranch and began to help out in the store. After Son Lee went back to Marathon, Glen took over management of the store. As personalities, Hallie and Glen were opposites. Hallie's cup was half-full; Glen's cup was half-empty. But Glen loved the Big Bend and was happy living there. In the past, she had earned her living as an accountant for a lumber firm, and she was a capable manager. The business did well, and in two years Hallie returned her nephew Bob's $5,000 gift with heartfelt thanks.

In 1978 Hallie retired from her job as justice of the peace and returned to the ranch to live out the remainder of her days. There were to be a good many of them and eventful ones, at that. Hallie moved into the room behind the store.

When Dadie retired from teaching in San Antonio, she and her husband, W. T. Potter, moved to Alpine. Once settled there, Dadie moved into the room behind the store, and W. T. went to the ranch on weekends. They purchased a large comfortable mobile home for Hallie and put it a short walk from the store. These were grander ranch digs than Hallie had ever imagined.

Guy continued to live at the old ranch headquarters. Son Stillwell lived in a mobile home placed at the end of the store property, as far as he could get from all the activity and still have access to running water and electricity. Once Dadie put me up to trying to encourage Son to retire from his construction business and spend his time just attending to ranching. By that time he was well over retirement age, and Hallie and Dadie were concerned for his health. Son told me that he didn't think he could hang around the ranch all day because too much petticoat government was involved. Hallie tartly reminded him that but for the petticoat government, there would be no ranch to hang around!

Dadie took over management of the store and RV park. Dadie was special magic. She welcomed each guest as if they were old friends, and in a few short years a great many of them were. No guest ever had a problem that was too minor to merit Dadie's attention. If Dadie were out of pocket, people postponed leaving until she returned so they could say goodbye. Snowbirds came and returned like swallows to Capistrano. Every guest had a story to tell about how Dadie had gone out of her way to make his or her visit to the Big Bend memorable.

One time a German couple had trouble with their motor home and had to be towed in to the RV park. This couple was spending a year touring the United States and Canada. They had shipped their motor home from Germany. It had been a special order from a German manufacturer and it was surely one of the grandest RVs ever to grace Stillwell Store and RV Park. However, evil spirits had fallen upon this grandeur, and the vehicle was diagnosed with a broken drive shaft. Using gestures, since the couple spoke limited English, the family's mechanics made the couple understand the seriousness of the problem, and that it's repair was beyond the locals' abilities. The repair shop in Marathon could do the work, but the problem was the broken drive shaft was foreign-made. Calls were placed to parts dealers, and it was soon determined that the part could be obtained from a Houston dealer, but it would have to be ordered. Delivery to

Houston would take three to four weeks, and another week to get it to the Big Bend.

The gentleman made several phone calls, speaking in German, and announced that he would "vait." Everyone connected to the RV park was amazed that this couple seemed unflappable over such a trying situation. The couple used the small car they were towing to sightsee for the next two days. They were having a delightful visit.

On the morning of the third day, a call came from Alpine that a Learjet had landed at the Alpine airport with an auto part and two German mechanics whose total English vocabulary consisted of "still" and "well." Someone went to get them, and the German mechanics repaired the motor home and left in their Learjet. The friendly couple departed, too, with appropriate *danke shön*.

Glen's health was failing, and her work had to be restricted to the morning hours. So Dadie's daughter Linda moved back to the ranch, down the road to her mobile home. Hallie continued with the business of being Hallie.

HALLIE THE CHILI QUEEN

From 1967 to the end of her life Hallie Crawford Stillwell reigned as queen of the Terlingua Chili Cook-off. She served as one of three judges at the first cook-off and this is the notation on the event from her files.

> One of my dear friends, H. Allen Smith, author of *Low Man on the Totem Pole*, was often considered a braggart among West Texans, but he was loved by all. He was the kind of person that knew a lot and he didn't mind telling you just how much he knew. Around West Texas, Smith was known as the chili king. No one could match his chili—not for taste, spice, or hotness.

> One day a newspaper reporter interviewed him and asked a lot of questions about his now-famous chili. Well, knowing Smith, I can easily guess what he said. "I make the world's best gol-darn chili. Can't nobody beat my chili and can't too many people eat my chili. In fact, my chili is the best in the world, and I dare anybody to challenge my chili."

> It seems that there was an Austin native named Wick Fowler who thought that his own chili was the best. He got wind of the declaration made by H. Allen Smith. Soon they were chunking threats back and forth through the media. A shoot-out would have to happen, and thus these two men originated the first chili cook-off in 1967. They haggled over

every detail. They threatened one another constantly while the location, date, and process were being established. Finally they agreed upon Terlingua, Texas, as a location. Terlingua was then a Brewster County quicksilver mining ghost town located about twenty minutes drive north of the Rio Grande. Of course this meant it was hours of driving from anywhere else, and participants would get there with maximum effort. The local population was estimated from nobody to two or three. The month would be October because the desert heat is unbearable before autumn. Even then we see temperatures rise into the triple digits most days. Soon the word was out and the contest was dubbed the "World Chili Cook-Off."

Judges were picked. H. Allen Smith picked me. Wick Fowler chose Floyd Schneider, vice president of the San Antonio Chamber of Commerce. (Some claimed he was bribed and paid well for his vote.) The third judge was David Witt, a Dallas attorney whom some regarded as the mayor of Terlingua.

Mud slinging increased on the day of the cook-off. Dallas newspaper columnist Frank X. Tolbert had written several articles promoting the event and Fowler's chili. Smith told me he caught Fowler's goon trying to put grasshopper legs in his chili. Fowler started a rumor that Smith was using beets and carrots in his chili. Fowler claimed a Texas hippie started the story. The contest was rising to its expectations.

When judging time came, I tasted first. I rolled the chili around my tongue, coughed several times, and swallowed hard. I drank two glasses of water after tasting Fowler's chili. Then I tried Smith's. It set my eyes to tearing and my nose to running. I savored the spices and tasted the flavor. It was awfully hot. I voted for H. Allen Smith.

Schneider did the same although I believed he cried more than I did. He voted for Fowler. Then David Witts stepped up to break the tie. He tasted both. He cried, coughed, sputtered and spit. He

couldn't handle the hot. He declared a mor?
for a year due to his burns stating, "It'll tak
for me to git back my taste buds. That stuff's ju…
darn hot!"

And so it was the first chili cook-off in Terlingua ended in a stalemate. No winner was declared. A second duel must be fought the next year. The 1968 Texas winner of the Terlingua Chili Cook-Off was Austin's Wick Fowler who became world famous with his 1, 2, and 3 Alarm Chili available from the grocery shelf even today. This second Terlingua event had come to a standoff between Fowler and California wine producer Woodruff (Wino Woody) De Silva. When the time came to open the ballot box, armed bandits appeared, stole the thing and made their escape. Calls for a voice vote by Referee Tolbert came to naught due, Tolbert claimed, to the reprehensible condition of the California judges. As opposed to the Texas judges, who, Tolbert observed, were models of sobriety.

Results of the 1969 Cook-Off would rock Terlingua and the nation. C. V. Woods, an Arizona planner and developer would topple the great Texas champion with a Green Napalm Chili, claimed by Fowler to have spinach in it.

But winners were to come in numbers from that day on. Queen Hallie kept on reigning. And every year she was presented with a new crown, each fashionably decorated with chili peppers. As time went by crowns began to stack up in her closet. And there were a few scepters lying here and there, too. One day Dadie noticed that bugs had invaded Hallie's closet. They were everywhere. Closer examination revealed that the royal regalia were the source of the problem. Dadie threw the stuff out.

Well, this did not at all suit the Queen, and she complained mightily. Nevertheless the bug-ridden finery stayed in the trash. The family told her that all queens, probably even Elizabeth and Neffertiti, from time to time find bugs in their crowns. It's just one of the hazards of the job!

So much has been written about the Terlingua Chili Cook-Offs that Hallie's story can add little to further enlighten. She loved the hoopla, and she was a tremendously good sport in wearing all the crazy crowns while holding up her end of the fun. She formed true friendships with New York humorist H. Allen Smith and his wife during the years they lived in Alpine. And she and Frank X. Tolbert delighted in each other's company. Mr. Tolbert took everything about chili seriously. He was a true connoisseur and poured scorn on those who put silly things in chili.

Hallie attended just about everything that went on in the Big Bend during the eighty-seven years she lived there. And in her gentle and humorous way she gave each event an added luster.

Queen Hallie and Her Chili Peppers Crown

Frank Tolbert

For the 11th straight year a judge will be crowned queen of the annual (and original) World Championship Chili Cookoff, this time on October 8 at Arribe (or upper) Terlingua, the next mining camp to Old Terlingua.

Our permanent queen is Judge Hallie Stillwell of Alpine, a lively and intelligent octogenarian who is the most beloved personality within the vast 6,204 square miles of Brewster County, Texas.

In a *Sports Illustrated* magazine story about the chili cookoff, Judge Stillwell was described as "the justice of the peace in Hell's Half Acre."

"And Hell's Half Acre isn't even in my precinct," said Hallie. "It's in Precinct 3 out of Marathon on the Gage Holland Ranch."

Hallie's Precinct 1 is about half the size of the State of Connecticut. She described it to me as "going south below the O2 ranch and the Kokernots (ranch) about 60 miles below Alpine, and just beyond Elephant Mountain and over to the Presidio County line."

Precinct 1 doesn't include the Terlingua-Study Butte-Arriba Terlingua triangle. However, Judge Stillwell is mighty popular in the country served by the Terlingua postoffice.

My daughter, Kathleen, makes a crown of red and yellow chili peppers for Judge Stillwell. And people who raise chiles around Arriba Terlingua contribute the peppers freely when they hear a crown will be fashioned for Hallie.

Judge Stillwell was married in 1918 to the late Roy Stillwell, who had ranches on both sides of the border. And Hallie still runs the historic Stillwell Ranch in Brewster County at the head of Maravillas Creek and near the start of 15-mile-long Shut Up Canyon through Stillwell Mountain.

There is also a Stillwell Crossing of the Rio Grande, but this is not on the ranch.

"When I was a bride in 1918 I got off to a bad start by washing the interior walls of the ranch house," said Hallie.

Hallie had been a schoolteacher in Marathon and Presidio before her marriage. And she didn't like what she took for ugly scribbling on the walls of her new home.

It turned out that this "ugly scribbling" was the ranch "books" and rainfall records inscribed there for decades by the Stillwell family.

"Roy was patient with me," said the judge. "But he did say that I erased a lot of history. He seemed especially sad to see the rainfall records gone."

The Villa de la Mina hotel at Arriba is already booked up for the weekend of the word championship. So is the nearby (35 miles) Big Bend National Park for the weekend of October 8–9.

You can stay in Alpine or Marfa, and there are still some vacancies (I think) at the new motel in Lajitas (Flat Rocks) just down the road toward Presidio from Arriba Terlingua.

Lajitas is on the Rio Grande near the mouth of Santa Elena canyon.

The new resort hotel at Lajitas is a reproduction of an old adobe fort once on the site. To make a reservation call Mrs. York at area code 713 and the number is 237-0851.

Each year the Texas State Championship Chili Cookoff for Women at Luckenbach names the competition for a great girl type of the past. For sample, last year's culinary tournament was called the Amelia Earhart Memorial.

The seventh annual in the series of cookoffs for female Texans only will be on Saturday, October 1. And Kathy Morgan, co-owner of Luckenbach, and other members of the sponsoring

Hell Hath No Fury Chili Society have announced that this will be the Annie Oakley Memorial.

Originally printed in the Dallas Morning News, *September 9, 1977. Thanks to Kathleen Tolbert Ryan and the* Dallas Morning News *for permission to reprint this article.*

Gubernatorial Declaration

WILLIAM P. CLEMENTS, JR.
Governor of Texas
AUSTIN, TEXAS

GREETINGS:

As Governor of Texas, I do hereby designate Saturday, November 7, 1981, as official Chili Day in Texas, being aware that this is also the date for the 15th annual renewal of the first chili cookoff in the world—now called the Wick Fowler Memorial World Championship.

The original happening took place in the autumn of 1967 and was created by Frank Tolbert and Tom Tierney in the ghost town of Terlingua, Brewster County, Texas on the Chirichura Ranch.

The first contest being between the late Wick Fowler of Austin–then chief cook of the Chili Appreciation Society International—and the late H. Allen Smith of Mount Kisco, New York. The match ended inconclusively when one of the judges choked on Smith's Yankee chili and was unable to cast a decisive vote for Fowler.

One cannot be a true son or daughter of the State without having his taste buds tingle at the thought of the treat that is real, honest-to-goodness, pure, unadulterated Texas chili.

As Governor, I am aware that Chili Day should be memorialized because that original cookoff 15 years ago on the Wills-Shelby Ranch has inspired a world-wide subculture dedicated to the appreciation of Texas chili con carne and expressed in more than 1,000 regularly scheduled chili cookoffs all over the world, from Bangkok, Thailand, to Rye, New York, to London and introducing thousands and thousands of persons to the delights of Texas-style chili con carne.

As Governor, I also remind Texas citizens that chili is the official State dish of Texas and I urge Texans to celebrate November 7, 1981, by enjoying a bowl of Texas-style chili on the date.

In official recognition whereof, I hereby affix my seal this 22nd day of October 1981.

PERSONAL REMINISCENCES

My Tribute to Hallie

Ken Ragsdale

I was one of Hallie's newer friends; our love affair began a mere thirty years ago. I well remember the day. We originally planned to meet for an interview on a Monday in Alpine, but since my schedule had changed, I called in advance to see if we could move the meeting up to Sunday afternoon. Hallie's response was pleasant, but firm: "No, Ken, it just won't work out. I go to church Sunday morning and play poker all Sunday afternoon. It'll just have to be Monday." And Monday it was.

During the ensuing thirty years Hallie and I met on many occasions for both business and pleasure. And each time when it was business, the meetings were a pleasure. The business was books. Hallie contributed to the three books I wrote on the Big Bend country. Thanks to Hallie, my books, her books, and other people's books with whom she also helped to write, leave an enduring legacy for generations to come. Through the printed word Hallie will live through the ages, inspiring others to live life to the fullest.

And she DID live life to the fullest. SHE DID IT ALL. She drove covered wagons, punched cattle, taught school within pistol shot of a Mexican revolution, owned and managed a ranch, survived drouth and depression, faced charging bulls and foreclosure-prone bankers, served as justice of the peace, jailed lawbreakers, and married eloping couples. She was a popular newspaper columnist, wrote books, delivered inspiring lectures, operated a trailer park and a trading post, and all the while remaining a lady of great eloquence, charm, and class.

And while Hallie traveled far and wide, home remained the ranch in her beloved Big Bend country. "There's something about ranch life that you don't give up," she once said. "Everything I ever did was for the ranch." And when I asked her if she didn't get lonely living in this remote section of Texas, she replied: "Lonely? Heavens, no. I'm never lonely as long as I can see the mountains." And so the mountains remain, along with our memories of Hallie.

Memories of Hallie. How can you think about Hallie without smiling? Some of the things she did as a judge—fined her own grandson for speeding, fined the mayor of Alpine $200 for DWI, and her best friend Inda Benson $25 for speeding. One of my favorite stories is about the time she tricked Tom Henderson into driving from Marathon down to the ranch, and then persuaded him to stay and help her lay new linoleum on the kitchen floor! Yet it fell to Tom to pay the great lady a most appropriate tribute: "Hallie Stillwell is what this country is all about. She's a legend here, an institution whose story would take a month of *Avalanches* to tell."

Quite true. And with that I'll say a final Adios, dear friend.

This tribute was originally written for Hallie's 90th birthday party. Kenneth Ragsdale's latest book, Big Bend Country: Land of the Unexpected *(College Station: Texas A&M University Press, 1998) includes a chapter on Hallie Stillwell. He is also author of several other books on the Big Bend.*

My First and Only Encounter with Judge Stillwell

Russ Gibson

My freshman year at Sul Ross State University began in 1971. I was nineteen years old and coming from a large city (Fort Worth). I found weekends to be somewhat boring in such a small town as Alpine. Still, I made some friends, and we spent time camping, mountain climbing, and driving across Paisano Pass to see the "Marfa Lights." There was a roadside park up there in the Davis

Mountains that we liked to visit to pass the time of day, enjoying the scenery and drinking beer.

As that second semester come to a close, a couple of friends and I went up there to celebrate the end of school. We went at night with a case of beer and sat in the car looking down on the lights of Alpine. We had made it through the first year of college!

As we drank, we chucked beer cans out of the window on the theory that if we were caught, we would have no evidence in the car. Those beer cans lying on the pavement could have been tossed there by anybody, or so we thought.

As you might guess, a Department of Public Safety trooper came along, and those guys do know the smell of beer. The fellow was pleasant and ever so gently inquired what we were doing. We said we were enjoying the breezes and the starlight. He agreed that it was a pleasant evening, and observed that he had stopped at this very place not two hours ago to enjoy the scene and that there were no beer cans on the pavement at that time. He wondered how they got there, located so close to our automobile and all.

Well, we could see that this was not his first rodeo and were not so foolish as to lie to a state trooper. We confessed. We were the ones who had tossed those beer cans out the window. He nodded amiably.

"In that case, you boys won't mind picking up those beer cans, will you?" he suggested, and of course we agreed. We picked them up all right, and when the trooper suggested we pick up every little bit of other trash in the park, the whole park and every square foot of it, we did not complain, figuring that our punishment would be a little bit of public service.

When we finished we reported back to the trooper, who had not gone away, but stood silently observing our labor. At that point we thought we were scot-free. The trooper thanked us for cleaning the park and said he would not cite us for littering, but he observed that by the light of the moon we looked awfully young. "You boys wouldn't be twenty-one would you?" "No sir," we said, knowing that the other shoe was about to drop.

He cited us for "minor-in-possession" and set up a court date in Alpine the following morning. Final exams were in a week, so we thought a little jail time might be used profitably to study up.

The next day we went to the courthouse and found ourselves standing before Judge Stillwell, a little old gray-haired lady with a kind face and a soft drawl. Well we thought we were in biscuits and gravy. This grandmother was not Roy Bean. She would go easy on us, being college boys with pretty faces.

She said, "I'm Judge Hallie Stillwell. Who might you boys be?" We introduced ourselves. She inquired as to the cause of our visit. She thought we might have a story or two to tell, and we did. We told the story, the whole story, and nothing but the story.

Judge Hallie raised an eyebrow, but said nothing. Underage drinking was common enough, but littering the sacred soil of Texas was rare enough that she had to open up her law books to find out the penalty. We looked at each other, each of us fearing the worst: Huntsville!

She found the appropriate statute, nodded, and banged her gavel. "Boys, that will be thirty days or thirty dollars." We lost no time paying the fine and started to leave, figuring we had been luckier than we deserved. Judge Hallie called out, as we were about to go through the door. I guess we looked pretty hangdog. "Don't feel bad, boys," she said. "My grandson had to face me last week on the same charges!"

It has now been a quarter of a century since I stood before Judge Hallie Stillwell and received my punishment. I never met her again, but I have always remembered that gray-haired old lady. She left a permanent impression in my memory. And I never messed with Texas again.

Miss Hallie's Walking Stick

Gardner Smith and Robert Reitz

Bob and I were soaking in the waters of Langford's Hot Spring down on the Rio Grande, not far above the Boquillas ferry, you probably know the place, when a couple of elderly gentlemen come down the sandy path and climbed in with us. They had been down to Heath Crossing earlier in the day to visit Andy Kurie and on the way back had stopped at the Stillwell Ranch to visit Miss Hallie. "Hallie Stillwell is still alive?" we inquired, incredulous. "Yes, indeed," the gentlemen exclaimed. She was as alive and sharp as a Spanish dagger they told us. We decided to go visit her, too, quite a trip from Langford's, as you must go around the Sierra Caballo Muerto, all the way north to the Chisos, then through Persimmon Gap of the Santiago Range, then come back around to the south again, down the draw of Maravillas Creek.

We had no trouble finding the Stillwell Ranch. It is a landmark almost as old as the Comanche occupation. This outfit lies to the east of Big Bend National Park. We have always come from the north or the West, from San Angelo, Odessa, or El Paso. We have never come from the East, from San Antonio or Del Rio, so have never visited the ranch. Still, everyone knows where the spread is located, filing away the directions for some future use, but as Santayana observes, the future is now.

We walked up to the porch of the Stillwell Store, where buttons of every description were happily munching on tacos and refried beans. It was hot enough to fry an egg on a rattlesnake's back but no one seemed to mind. The kids were as happy as kids are ever likely to be, at least West of the Pecos.

We went in the store. This is an old-fashioned kind of general store with all the things that Western folks are likely to need. We introduced ourselves to Dadie Potter, Miss Hallie's daughter, and said we'd like to pay our respects to the Great Lady. Hats in hand, we were politely asked to wait a moment while Dadie went to inquire whether Hallie could see us just then. Dadie returned in a moment and we followed her into Hallie's study adjacent to the store, and we were introduced the old fashioned way: "Mr. Smith and Mr. Reitz from Oak Cliff."

We shook her weathered old hand and waited to be invited to take our seats. There were ten thousand things we wanted to ask her, but we knew a dozen or so was all we could hope for. It was kind of like a first date.

We asked about Oscar and Bessie Langford, first of all, for she knew them personally. We told her we had just come up from the Langford's Hot Spring, and she nodded. Membership in Club West Texas requires a soak in that spring for admission.

Miss Hallie liked Bessie a lot. She had true grit, she said, but she didn't care much for Oscar. "He wasn't a rancher," she said, not with malice, just matter of fact. We're not ranchers either, but we're her guests. "He was. . ." she searched for just the right word, the schoolteacher in her coming out, ". . . parsimonious." "Yet thrift is a virtue," I gently reminded her. "Yes," she said with a

117

wave of her hand. There was an uncomfortable silence. She knows what's real and what's not. The land is real, nothing else.

After an hour we figured we were getting close to wearing out our welcome. Many people come to visit Hallie Stillwell. Just then the range boss came in to give her a hug and a kiss. He had just come back from escorting a party of visitors down Maravillas Canyon and he lost some of them. "They just slipped off," he admitted. He was going back down to look for them after a little supper.

I went back into the store to get a couple of her books from the pile on the counter, and I asked her to autograph them, which she did. She asked us for the date. I said that we had been out in the desert for a week and had kind of lost track. "Let's call it the twenty-sixth then," she said, and we agreed. It was good enough by the way time in the Big Bend is reckoned. I help open the front free endpaper to read the inscription. Hallie has such beautiful handwriting and I complimented her on it. "I was a schoolteacher, young man, " is what she said. Old enough to have taught my mother, she called me 'young man,' I who have enjoyed forty-five springtimes, and the same number of autumns.

Hallie Stillwell was a judge up in Alpine for fourteen years, from 1962 to 1977. Sometimes she was called upon to render judgment on her own kin. That clear, penetrating look she has may disarm some, but I've seen it before. My grandmother would have been nearly Miss Hallie's age had she lived, and I knew my grandmother, too. Some of my best lessons in what's right and what's wrong were received at the hands of old ladies. So I'm comfortable with Miss Hallie and Bob is too, for judge she does — seeing what kind of metal we are made of. Her glance read our brands before we even took our seats. Out in the desert for ten days, we were not looking our Sunday best, but Miss Hallie has judged men not by their looks but by their character all of her life. We sat transfixed by the old lady's stories of those who lived by good and those by greed. Miss Hallie is a link to the past—a link forged by the strong desert sun.

Roy Stillwell, Hallie Crawford's choice in marriage, passed in 1948. We knew that of course. We were babes of two at that time. We were not about to ask about it, but she told us about that day anyway. Roy was a lot older than Hallie and naturally might have expected to spin off this mortal coil while she was still alive, but in a land full of real hazards—rattlesnakes and scorpions, falling

118

rocks and flash floods and cattle stampedes Roy turned his truck over one night coming home after a day of work. We expressed our condolences. We guessed she had gotten over it, but you never know. She might still awaken in the night and ask Roy to get her a glass of water.

After a respectful pause I asked, to change the subject away from something so painful, if the Big Bend Stillwells were kin to Vinegar Joe Stilwell. Well, her eyes lit up and she told us the story. Yes, she said, Joe Stilwell was a distant cousin, though that branch of the family spelled their name with three ells instead of four. She gave a big old chuckle and told of how in 1948, wearing her widow's weeds, she caught the Southern Pacific for a trip up to New York City. Well, when the conductor found out her name was Stillwell he brought her up the to the VIP Pullman and showered her with courtesies. "I rode in considerable style," she said. Eventually she discovered it was a case of mistaken identity. "They thought I was Vinegar Joe's widow," she gasped through her laughter, and we laughed out loud as well. Everything turns out right in the end, laughing with the dead, who just love to laugh and hardly ever get the chance.

Dadie looked in to see what all the laughter was about and we figured that was the time to say our goodbyes, so we did, shaking the frail old hand again, not knowing what to say, for perhaps we would see her again only in heaven (though as it turned out we visited her twice again in subsequent years). We stepped back out into the evening sun, not saying much, but we looked at each other and nodded, having just experienced one of those defining moments in life which come very seldom. When we stand at heaven's gates, Miss Hallie will be waiting there, saying "Let them in, Pete. They weren't ranchers but they knew how to laugh."

Dadie followed us out and asked where we were camping that night. We hadn't given a thought, we never do, just plopping down wherever we happen to find ourselves. "Well, we have a spare trailer" she offered, "and since this is Saturday night we could show a movie out on the porch come sundown." How could we refuse?

Come sundown we all, friends, guests, family, and tumbleweeds, settled down on the porch to watch the movie — one in which Miss Hallie is featured — Bandits, Bootleggers, and Businessmen. And Miss Hallie herself sat on the porch with us. A legend in her own time, more than one chapter in the story of the West was written by Hallie Stillwell.

The next morning we rose early, but not as early as Hallie and her daughter. "We have water now," said Dadie with a sigh. "But it won't last all summer." It's a big ranch so they've got water elsewhere in springs and tinajas and wells, but the cattle, poor dumb beasts, have got to drink too and they'll have to send a man way out back to spend a whole day filling the water truck and bring it down. It's just one of many prices you pay for your solitude.

We wondered if Miss Hallie ever got tired of folks asking "Tell us about this and tell us about that?" No she does not. Folks have come a long way to visit her, and she respects that. It's an investment in knowledge. We live in an age when hardly anyone wants to know how things were long ago. Those who do, come here: like pilgrims to a Zen Master seeking truth. Hallie Stillwell is a woman with her entire life behind her, all but a few grains of sand. Her life behind her, she gives a few grains of sound advice! All of life behind her, but for us, these are still the good old days. Oh, should we be so fortunate to bask in the glow of old age's desert sun.

With equal grace Miss Hallie lends her name to both chili festivals in Big Bend every year. There's one for men over in Terlingua, or rather Villa de las Minas (the bare-breasted babes being mere ornament); and the women's chili festival, "Hell Hath No Fury Like a Woman Scorned Chili Festival, No Men Allowed." It's all in good fun. Men and women really do need to sleep in separate beds from time to time. In any event, no one ever scorned Miss Hallie: it's yes ma'am and no ma'am from all alike.

After we had slaked our thirst for water, we kicked back and enjoyed those old Big Bend breezes. I asked Bob what the next plane of existence might be for us. He thought a moment and said, "Given half a chance I'd come back as Miss Hallie's walking stick."

Miss Hallie was, as our friend Gerald Vance once said, "There when they brought in the dirt." Miss Hallie hails from the Cambrian family — solid bedrock. Long after the adobe walls have melted away, Miss Hallie will walk these desert hills with her sotol walking stick.

Gardner Smith and Robert Reitz are authors of three books on the Big Bend:
Thunder in the Chisos *(Oak Cliff, Texas: The Sun and Shadow Press, 1989),*
Big Solitude *(Oak Cliff, Texas: The Sun and Shadow Press, 1991), and* Western
Habits *(Oak Cliff, Texas: The Sun and Shadow Press, 1994).*

Bride Scrubbed off Ranch's Records

Frank X. Tolbert

Mrs. Hallie Stillwell, one of the great ladies of the Big Bend, lives in Alpine (where she's justice of the peace) but spends as much time as she can on the Stillwell Ranch, near Stillwell Mountain and the Stillwell Crossing of the Rio Grande.

Years ago, when she came to the ranch as a bride, though, there was a real crisis. Young Mrs. Stillwell noticed that there "was a lot of scribbling" on the interior walls of the ranch house, especially on the door faces and window frames.

"I'd been taught not to write on the wall," she said. So, without consulting her husband, the late Roy Stillwell, she washed the walls clean of all the writing.

Roy wasn't happy when he came home that evening from a hard day on the range and found the walls clean. "For it turned out that I'd washed away all the ranch records for years," said Mrs. Stillwell. "Roy kept his books on the ranch house walls, and things like the registration of pure bred calves and the amounts of rain that had fallen on the ranch for years and years. Roy was patient with me, but he was especially saddened to lose those rainfall records. 'How am I going to win any bets now' he said to me."

I told Mrs. Stillwell about a near-disaster when the late Bill Edwards lost his hat. Old Bill had, up until a few years ago, a huge ranch near Fort Stockton (about sixty miles north of Alpine). And I used to visit him occasionally. He kept all his ranch records inscribed on the brims of his droopy old sombrero. The hat had several brims to accommodate years of records. There was hell to pay around the Edwards ranch when he lost his hat somehow, but it was finally found.

This recollection is from Tolbert's Texas column in the November 9, 1968 edition of the Dallas Morning News. *Thanks to the News and Kathleen Tolbert Ryan for permission to reprint it.*

Dirty Woman Creek Isn't Named For Hallie

Frank X. Tolbert

A single sinkhole in the headwaters of Dirty Woman Creek may have inspired the name of the stream long ago, Judge Hallie Stillwell says.

Anyway, it is known that wives of Terlingua miners in the old days took dips in this natural bathing place.

Dirty Woman Creek flows only when it rains and is mostly a nuisance, especially in Old Terlingua, because of its deep, rocky channel. The sinkhole in Sawmill Canyon usually has some water in it, however, even during droughts.

Judge Stillwell, owner of the historic Stillwell Ranch, became interested in Dirty Woman Creek several years ago when jokers started spreading the report that the creek was named for her.

She is the co-author, with Virginia Madison, of a book on the nomenclature of landmarks in the wild country of the Big Bend. There is no mention of Dirty Woman Creek in the book.

Virginia Madison and other friends of Hallie Stillwell were concerned that gossip of the creek's title was a reference to the judge. They persuaded another friend, Gene Hendryx of Alpine, then a member of the State Legislature, to push through a resolution declaring that Judge Stillwell did not inspire the stream's unflattering name.

Hallie Stillwell is easily one of the most beloved citizens in the 6,204 square miles of Brewster County.

For 17 years, before each Terlingua cook-off my children, Frank No. 2, Kathleen, and Ann—have made a crown of chili peppers for Hallie Stillwell. She is the permanent chili queen of the Original Terlingua Chili Appreciation Society International Cookoff.

Kathleen once made the crown on cook-off morning, and she tried to buy some fresh red and green chiles at Arturo White's Terlingua Store. When Mrs. White was told that the peppers would be used to make a tiara for Judge Stillwell, she told Kathleen, "There is no charge if they are for Queen Hallie. And I hope she will be here for many more crownings."

Dallas Morning News, *November 6, 1983. At the time this was written there were two Original Terlingua Chili Appreciation Society Cookoffs, staged on the same day and only four miles apart. Carroll Shelby hosted the other one. Shelby and Tolbert cooked up the first one in 1967. Thanks to the* News *and Kathleen Tolbert Ryan for permission to reprint this article.*

The Myth. . .
About Hallie and Guns and
Controversial Matters

Betty Heath

Guns figured largely in everyday life in the Big Bend and in pioneer days, and they figured no more and no less in Hallie's life than anyone else's who lived where she lived and did what she did. When Hallie rode out to check the cattle, her rifle was attached to her saddle. When Hallie was at home, tending her family, cooking her meals, cleaning her house, her rifle was at the ready. I can remember that a very large revolver hung on a nail high above the back door of the ranch house. Its purpose was for the use of whoever had to go to the outhouse. We children couldn't just go to the outhouse. We had to find an adult to accompany us. This adult would go ahead of us and shoot the rattlesnakes, which had sought the shelter and shade of the outhouse. The Stillwell-Crawford children learned to plan ahead.

When Hallie began her lecture tours in the 1950s, a desperate measure to make money to hold on to the ranch, she took her props which consisted of rifles, revolvers, lariats, tack, and gear. These items, so everyday to those of us who used them, were exotic curiosities to the Marion Morrison generation. Mr. Morrison, of course, became John Wayne, who came to believe in his own myth. Hallie Stillwell started out as Hallie Stillwell, and Hallie Stillwell she remained. She didn't need a myth, she just needed money to feed the cows and pay the damn taxes. I suspect that Hallie patterned her lecture style after our cousin, Bert Davis. Bert owned a tent show back in the 1920s. He had lived in Central America for a short time, and Bert spun wonderful tales. Son and Guy were absolutely fascinated by him. He was tall and stately. He dressed in white linen and looked more like Buffalo Bill than Buffalo Bill did. Bert is a subject for a whole other book. Suffice it to say that the colleges and clubs who paid Hallie to come and lecture did not pay for a dull time, and Hallie did not give them one. She didn't have to embroider her stories, but the tales she told in the fifties were largely about events that happened in the late teens and early twenties of the century. No longer were the ranch families being raided and murdered by marauders. They still carried guns, and defended themselves against the predators, four-footed, two-footed, and no-footed.

Both Hallie and Dadie were experts in weaponry. They had been taught to be, and they won so many "turkey shoots" that they were no longer permitted to compete. Hallie used her gun to defend her cattle against predators and to take game for feeding the family. Beyond that Hallie didn't give guns a lot of thought. And I think it is safe to say that by Charlton Heston's standards, she never owned a decent one. It's a miracle she ever hit anything.

In the latter part of Hallie's life, some reporter was always calling her and asking what she thought of the possibility of reintroducing wolves in the National Park area.

Hallie didn't fail to tell them. I used to pray for the telephone service to dysfunction. It seems to go out after every rain, but never when you most want it to.

Hallie had great respect, but not a lot of sympathy, for the predatory animals. Simply put, it was a matter of who was going to survive, and Hallie intended it to be the Stillwell Ranch.

An End and a Beginning

As the curtain falls upon this drama of a well-lived life, I can hardly convince myself that the play is over. The lead characters have gone home. And so must the bit players and the audience.

Son Stillwell died at the end of 1998. By the end of another year, Guy was gone. And then Dadie passed away in the spring of 2001.

In the end it was Dadie who saved the ranch. Guy had sold his interest when he was no longer able to be an active rancher. Dadie bought Son's interest when his health failed, and in doing so saved the greater portion of what Hallie called "Roy's Dream."

The dream goes on in the persons of Dadie's four surviving children, Kay Pizzini, Linda Perron, Nannette Patton, and Travis Potter and their families. "Nothing lasts forever," say our seers, soothsayers, and prophets, and Lord knows there's ample proof of that. But the Stillwell Ranch will probably go on a while longer. Dadie's heirs love that patch of desert every bit as much as those who came before them. The ranch is in their very blood. Their ambition, one and all, is to complete their careers and endeavors and get back to the ranch. And the next generation seems to share their attachment. All told, prospects look pretty good down there. Benevolent spirts no doubt beam down upon them from "*el otro lado.*"